THE FARMER'S FRIEND

The
FARMER'S
FRIEND

OR

WISE SAWS &
MODERN INSTANCES

BEING

A Collection of Country Sayings
compiled and commented upon by

W. S. MANSFIELD
Director of Cambridge University Farm

with 4 illustrations

CAMBRIDGE
AT THE UNIVERSITY PRESS
1947

CAMBRIDGE
UNIVERSITY PRESS

University Printing House, Cambridge CB2 8BS, United Kingdom

Published in the United States of America by Cambridge University Press, New York

Cambridge University Press is part of the University of Cambridge.

It furthers the University's mission by disseminating knowledge in the pursuit of education, learning and research at the highest international levels of excellence.

www.cambridge.org
Information on this title: www.cambridge.org/9781107629479

© Cambridge University Press 1947

First published 1947
First paperback edition 2014

A catalogue record for this publication is available from the British Library

ISBN 978-1-107-62947-9 Paperback

PREFACE

The country sayings that I have commented upon in this book have been drawn from many sources, the majority of them directly from farmers, though a few which were new to me I have found in books, particularly some in that charming little book by Colonel C. N. French, *A Countryman's Day Book*, published by Dent in 1929.

No doubt there are many different versions of most of them, and I do not claim that mine is the original and authentic version. Still less do I claim that my interpretations are the only ones that could be given.

About fifty of these sayings, with my commentaries, have already appeared in *Country Life*, and I am greatly indebted to the publishers of that paper, and to its Editor, Mr Frank Whitaker, for permission to reproduce them here.

I have slipped in a number of saws on the weather; but I am no meteorologist, and I have not ventured to comment upon these. I believe my readers will be as grateful as I am to Mr Kendon for his introduction and to Mr John Hookham for his drawings.

W. S. M.

UNIVERSITY FARM
CAMBRIDGE
October 1946

INTRODUCTION

The fool has his compensations, as the ass his ears. Notoriety is better than nonentity—it is at least evidence of character. William Blake wrote: *If the fool would persist in his folly he would become wise.*

Solomon and his peers, of course, have no time or respect for fools. Yet folly and wisdom are sometimes near neighbours: the one does not know that a matter is important, the other knows that it is not important. The resulting peace of mind or happy satisfaction in themselves they share laughing. What label would apply to the countryman who says, as he moistens the palms of his hands: 'That don't take *us* long to do a five-minutes job'? Or to the other who, having emptied the swill in the trough, leans over the gate of the sty to meditate: 'I reckon they pigs be rightly named'? Is it altogether a condemnation, that a fool and his money are soon parted, when Solomon himself declared that the love of money is the root of all evil? Shakespeare loved fools, and gave them good parts, and made them wise in their own way. There were more fools in the world in Shakespeare's day than in Solomon's. More still, in ours.

I have thought, it takes a fool to make a good proverb. For the fool is never cool and cautious. Where a wiseacre might noddingly say, *Concentration of effort is one of the secrets of success*, a fool cries, *Rolling stones gather no moss*. He cares about the vividness and leaves the wisdom to his audience. Proverbs are often about fools, for the fool is like a Scot in this (this only) that he enjoys a joke against himself. It is the fool's bliss that he knows himself for a fool, not only accepting but actively corroborating the wise world's poor opinion of him. He accepts his folly, and for our benefit puts it to use in proverbs. The wise man who thinks himself wise is a trap for himself and his disciples, but the chap who knows he is a fool is the safest of all company.

The finest and wisest fools live out in the country, there to remain the townsman's best butts. These odd fellows—who will spend good-morning and good-night upon anyone, whether they know him or not, who even like rain at times, and look at the sun to tell if it's dinner-time, who move so slowly (and get so much work done, *considering*), who cannot lie abed in daylight—these are a secretive, roughly dressed race, showing even more than the usual human inclination to poetry (irrational by definition) in their resort to sidelong and picturesque forms of expression. No doubt it is still true to say that the acres of England are rich in fools, if you take care to get your definition right.

In this little pocket book Mr Mansfield has collected some of the countryman's wild and cryptic sayings, those, particularly, that are concerned with the mysteries of farming. By a kindly betrayal, Mr Mansfield now makes plain, even to townsmen, what each old fellow once wrapped up whimsically in a kind of wit to please himself and to hide from all but the initiates. *Sheep should never hear the church bells twice in the same field*, is useful knowledge in a delightfully memorable form for those who can profit by it; so is

> *Fetlock, feet, and feather,*
> *Tops may come, but bottoms never.*

The canny townsman won't make much of this wisdom, though it would clinch an argument in *The Bushel and Strike*, where it would sort the company into the knowing and the ignorant. 'Tis a very odd—not to say foolish—way of saying what it has to say. What it has to say is valuable, but it isn't (or it wasn't till Mr Mansfield came along) wisdom to be handed out to an anybody. The dictionary may tell a wise one what *fetlock* is; it will not help him much with *tops* and *bottoms*.

As a bible text to a puritan so is a proverb to a country-man; it ends argument, puts, as some say, a stopper in it. And there lurks a danger. Proverbs are rule-of-thumb wisdom, picturesque withal, and they have a neat trick of by-passing the Reason. I have not consulted Mr Mansfield, but I think I may say I have personal evidence that indecision and laziness are inborn in the human race; and, as life consists of a series of decisions, it is not to be wondered at that any simple mechanism (such as a proverb) for arriving at a decision without the labour of deciding, is gladly accepted. Hence the invariable and delightful downrightness of proverbs and such sayings. *A bird in the hand is worth two in the bush*, is, for instance, so downright and yet so unsound a rule for stock-exchange operators that unless some of them acted according to some other proverb (say: *Faint heart never won fair lady*) speculation would die out, and what has hitherto been known as civilization would succumb; and we don't want it to do that!

Proverbs, however, are not universal maxims; and those who take them to be so have only themselves—not the proverbs—to blame. A true proverb advertises its proverbial character by a beautiful element of ambiguity. Trying to nail down the precise meaning of a proverb is as tormenting as trying to catch a bluebottle on a window-pane. Let the reader try his mind upon this one:

> *He that buys land buys many stones,*
> *He that buys flesh buys many bones,*
> *He that buys eggs buys many shells,*
> *He that buys good ale buys nothing else.*

There is a sense in which this sounds like a commendation of ale-buyers; conceivably it might be used by brewers for encouragement of customers; but what should be the exact cast of countenance to accompany the last three words? Might not the rhyme also come in usefully in a temperance oration? What exactly might one mean by it, for instance, in reciting it to a tipsy thatcher?

Or another example from Mr Mansfield's bag—what would be the rock-bottom meaning of this?—

> *Children and chicken*
> *Must always be picking.*

Mr Mansfield reads it as an injunction, and justifies it; but there lingers about it, for one reader at least, the sound of a sarcastic female voice whose other favourite outlet was *Little pigs have big ears.* The most characteristic proverbial sayings seem to be those that have the widest possibilities in this way; they no more than have a *tendency* to mean something. Dropped into talk concerned with particular circumstance, they take their specific meaning, just then, from what goes on when and whereabouts they are quoted.

Farmers are not the race to take advice easily. Scorn for my ignorance is stronger in them than respect for my knowledge, unless I speak in proverbs, when it seems I speak according to the common consent of countrymen.

> *A plant a stride:*
> *Let un bide.*

If I can say that, gravely, as we lean over the gate above the mangolds, chewing our bents, of a Sunday, I shall pass muster. It won't be much of a crop, as he knows I know, but it will be less of a loss than if he ploughed them in. But to be ignorant, and willing to learn, is to be in an even better state. A mild pleasant day or two in January may tempt an ignoramus to nod 'nice weather' to a knowing one. 'I don't like it myself' he retorts. 'My father used to say,

> *If you see grass in January*
> *Lock your grain in your granuary.'*

And I am pleased to be contradicted with so kind a citation. Thus proverbism settles many an uneasy matter—a good neutralizer for acidity.

Mr Mansfield does not find, that modern knowledge in agriculture always enforces the adage. There is (for instance) a good deal about the moon which science now bids us reject.

The moon cannot be relied upon in waxing or waning; she has, they say, no effect upon weather and none upon fertility. Even lunatics are named by a misapprehension. Nevertheless, old beliefs die hard. Science may be right, or science may not be right, 'all I know is', as the gardener says, 'The wind'll change with the moon, and when that change we'll get the wet, and not before'. Moreover, one important thing for gardeners and farmers and all who have to do with the multitudes of slow processes of earth, and season, is that they should have a definite calendar; one that reminds them, and sets them busy in spite of themselves. It may be superstition to sow beans on St Valentine's Day or plant potatoes on Good Friday; but it is science to get them in at just such a time as shall be neither too early nor too late, and (making the worst of it) if superstition gets the beans in successfully at such a time, why superstition, in this, does no harm. When all's said and done, it will, I suspect, be matter for surprise (though it ought not to be) that modern science is able to approve and to reinforce so many of the picturesque proverbs of experience. If we are surprised, is not this because, just now, with penicillin on the right hand and atom bombs on the wrong, a proverbless generation is too apt to regard science itself as a supplanting mystery and scientists as its priests. But science is younger than wisdom and vision, and Reason is still at school under Experience. At great cost of time and money a research worker was once instructed to find out by science the best possible method of drying hops. His five-year conclusion was, that the traditional process easily produced the best hops for their job. No doubt the old process was slow, wasteful of labour, more costly; but the speedier, more saving methods inevitably lost something which it had been the prime care of the 'unscientific' hop dryer to preserve. Who knows what knowledge, what experiment, what intuition were at work in the craftsmen, to give them guidance along a path with an infinity of side-turnings? No doubt but *we* are the people, and wisedome shall die with us. But trial and error, helped out by dogged cogitation and daring imagination, are old names for what the scientist calls experiment and deduction. 'We shall do 'er, 'low us time.' No one knows the wild progenitor of wheat; no one knows the history of its patient breeding; but it is certain that such a plant did not come, and survive, by chance. If not, then it came by knowledge, skill, and patience, which we now call science. Some of this is embalmed in the country sayings of the world, where Poetry and Knowledge have accorded and kissed. As Blake began, so let him end, with this mystery from the Proverbs of Hell: *If others had not been foolish, we should be so.*

FRANK KENDON

WISE SAWS AND MODERN INSTANCES

BAKED MEAT IS BETTER THAN BOILED

This is supposed to explain the well-known fact that cattle will not thrive nearly so well during a wet grazing season as during a comparatively dry one, though it is not suggested that the explanation was ever intended to be taken seriously. There are, however, several good reasons to account for the phenomenon, though at first sight it seems extraordinary that in seasons when grass is plentiful cattle do not do so well as when it is short. In a wet season, however, the grass tends to grow *away* from the cattle rather than grow *to* them, with the result that much of it soon becomes old, fibrous and of lower nutritive value. In extreme cases it may even get away to such a degree that it sends up flowering shoots, at which stage its feeding value is lower still. When cattle are wandering about in grass up to their hocks it is certain that they are not doing as well as they should. Again in such a season, owing to the nature of the grass, the cattle are continually scouring, their food does not 'stay by them' and they fail to put on weight. Exactly the opposite is to be seen in a very dry season, when it is remarkable how well the cattle thrive, even though there seems to be very little for them to eat at all. Presumably what there is is highly nutritious and the cattle make the best possible use of it. As another old saw puts it: 'The milk comes from the grass you can't see.'

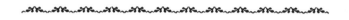

FAT HORSES SPELL FOUL FARMS

This saw obviously dates from the pre-tractor era, when all the work on a farm was done by horses, and in those days it may well have been true. A fat horse does not mean a fit horse; there is a world of difference between the two. A fat horse is an idle horse, and if the horses have been idle there is little chance of the land having been properly cultivated. But though fat horses may generally have meant foul farms it does not follow that foul farms meant fat horses—in fact generally the reverse—for on most foul and poverty-stricken farms the horses were underfed and overworked, being too few in number. 'Feed them well and work them hard' is still the golden rule for the management of farm horses.

UNLESS YOUR BACON YOU WOULD MAR,
KILL NOT YOUR PIG WITHOUT THE R

For the home curing of bacon this is no doubt excellent advice, though under modern factory conditions bacon is successfully cured all the year round.

HE THAT BUYS,
OUGHT TO HAVE A HUNDRED EYES

Caveat emptor!

HE THAT BUYS LAND BUYS MANY STONES,
HE THAT BUYS FLESH BUYS MANY BONES;
HE THAT BUYS EGGS BUYS MANY SHELLS,
HE THAT BUYS GOOD ALE BUYS NOTHING ELSE

There are at least two possible inferences, the first that though there are drawbacks in purchasing most things there are none in purchasing ale, because the buyer gets ale unadulterated (though even years ago it presumably contained at least 90 per cent of water), or alternatively that ale is poor value for money.

But I like the wit of a third significance even better—that the ale-bibber (to adapt a biblical compound noun) has money for nothing but ale.

A CHERRY YEAR, A MERRY YEAR,
A PLUM YEAR, A DUMB YEAR

A rhyme without reason, or at least without any that I can fathom.

Change of weather finds discourse for fools

ON YOUR FARM AT CANDLEMAS DAY, SHOULD BE HALF THE STRAW AND TWO-THIRDS OF THE HAY

Candlemas is 2 February, and, as the adage suggests, the hungriest months of the year are yet to come. Grass cannot be counted on until May, and, though in some seasons it may be three weeks earlier, in others it may be three weeks later. Hence the prudent and far-sighted farmer will make provision for a late spring. Quite apart from this consideration is the desirability of improving the quality of the food as the winter advances. When the cattle come into their winter quarters, straw may be fed with only a small proportion of hay. Later on, however, the diet should be improved by increasing the proportion of hay. It is a common mistake to start feeding hay too soon, thus using the best of the food during the first part of the winter with nothing so good with which to follow on.

IT'S A POOR PROSPECT FOR ANY PARISH WHEN THE DOGS IN IT OUTNUMBER THE SHEEP

If this be true then the outlook for many parishes is black indeed, for there must be thousands without a single sheep! But I fancy it only refers to those parishes in the south, south-east and east where there are large areas of light arable land, where the soils are often shallow, and where the traditional way of maintaining fertility was by means of folding sheep. Unfortunately, as the result of economic conditions, this system of farming began to decline soon after the end of the 1914–18 war, and ever since then the number of flocks has steadily decreased, the pace of their disappearance having only been accelerated by the recent war. There are those who maintain that ultimately it will be found impossible to farm this kind of land without sheep; on the other hand, there are those who claim that they can maintain soil fertility perfectly well in other ways. Who are right only time can tell, but it is rather significant that where the Excess Profits Tax allows the luxury of indulging in uneconomic enterprises, sheep are again making an appearance on farms where they have not been seen for many years.

HALF THE PEDIGREE GOES IN AT THE MOUTH

This saw embodies a profound truth or an equally profound fallacy, depending upon how it is interpreted; though the correct interpretation is perhaps the obvious one. The perfect animal is the result of a combination of good breeding and good feeding. No young animal can develop the potentialities of its breeding unless it is given the opportunity of doing so by being reared on a high plane of nutrition. The best bred calf in the world will grow into something little better than a scrub if it is raised on a starvation diet. No amount of good feeding that it may subsequently receive will alter it; hence the justification for the high plane of nutrition upon which young pedigree animals—particularly young males destined for stock purposes—are raised. Unless young stock are so reared, unless they are given the opportunity of developing the potentialities of their breeding, it is impossible to tell which, if any, possess these potentialities at all, and impossible for the breeder to exercise selection. This necessity of the pedigree breeder so to rear his young stock has always been recognized, and it is interesting to reflect that the work of Robert Bakewell—that great pioneer of livestock improvement—would have been impossible had he been born fifty years earlier, before the introduction of the root crop into English farming. It cannot be over-emphasized that the rearing of young pedigree stock on a high plane of nutrition —a practice that is often ignorantly criticized—has sound scientific justification.

This does not mean that it is necessary or even desirable to keep mature animals in high condition. It is often said that fat can cover a multitude of faults, and so no doubt it can, particularly from the eyes of the inexperienced. But this has nothing whatever to do with the principle of rearing young stock on a high plane of nutrition, and is beside the point.

The saw is false, however, if it is interpreted as meaning that the nutrition that an animal receives has any influence upon its genetic make-up. Such an idea is of course absurd, for that is something which is settled once and for all at the time of conception, long before the animal is even born. The plane of nutrition upon which a young dairy bull is reared cannot in any way influence the milking qualities of the daughters he begets. At first sight this would seem to neutralize the argument which has been already used in favour of raising young bulls on a high plane of nutrition.

6

The argument is of course much stronger when applied to beef bulls, where the important qualities that are being aimed at are visible, rather than to dairy bulls where they are invisible. Yet even with dairy bulls there are strong arguments in favour of rearing them well; otherwise if they grow into ugly, malformed creatures it will not be known if their misfortune is the result of malnutrition or heredity.

It is interesting to note that the rearing of young stock on a high plane of nutrition was one of Tusser's five hundred points of good husbandry:

> 'Pinch never thy wennels of water or meat,
> If ever ye hope to have them good neat.'

WHAT GROWS IN MAY SHOULD BE EATEN IN MAY

This old maxim, familiar to all graziers, embodies the scientific truth that the nutritive value of grass is highest when it is young and leafy. If grass is under-grazed in May it will send up flowering shoots in June and become woody and indigestible, and the protein content will fall markedly. The aim of good grazing is to keep the grass in the young leafy state. This will be impossible unless it is kept closely grazed in the early part of the season. As the season advances, however, the difficulty becomes less, for the tendency of the grass to send up flowering shoots is reduced, until eventually—probably by August—the grass shows little further inclination to send up flowering shoots and the growth from that date onwards will tend to be of the desirable leafy character.

One of the greatest criticisms that could be offered of the management of our pastures in this country as a whole in the pre-war years was the extent of the under-grazing. In Romney Marsh, where much of the grassland was most skilfully managed for the purpose of sheep-grazing, the test of good grazing was claimed to be that a sixpence thrown 20 yards could be found again without difficulty.

ONE YEAR'S SEEDING
SEVEN YEARS' WEEDING

This to-day is an understatement, for, in spite of all the facilities that our modern machinery gives us for numerous and rapid cultivations, and in spite of all our new spraying techniques, which are an immense help both in weed-prevention as well as in weed-eradication, it is doubtful if any method is as effective as the old-fashioned way of hand weeding. Long ago when labour was cheap and plentiful—when, for example, at a day's notice a gang of fifty or more women and children could be mobilized to pull charlock at a trivial cost—it was possible to keep the land cleaner than it is to-day, notwithstanding all our modern methods. This is not to decry these methods, for without them we should be in a bad way. But we must recognize that our forefathers were much better able to deal with a field where weeds had been allowed to seed than we are to-day. Even they considered that it would take seven years to clean. It certainly will not take less time now.

SOW PEAS AND BEANS IN THE WANE OF THE MOON
WHO SOWETH THEM SOONER HE SOWETH TOO SOON

The belief that the phase of the moon at the time of sowing is important and affects the subsequent growth of the crop was once universal and still persists in some degree particularly among gardeners, though none of those I know who believe in it are able to explain to me why, or even what the different effects precisely are. Tusser says:

> 'That they, with ye planet, may rest and rise,
>   And flourish with bearing most plentiful wise.'

In a note in *Tusser Redivivus* published in 1744 the author adds: 'Peas and beans sown during the increase do run more to hawm and straw; and during ye declension, more to cod, according to the common consent of countrymen.'

PLOUGH DEEP WHILE SLUGGARDS SLEEP
AND YOU SHALL HAVE CORN TO SELL AND KEEP

Or alternatively

> 'There is no gain without pain,
>   Then plough deep while sluggards sleep.'

There has lately been a good deal of discussion as to the merits of deep ploughing, and a great many carefully controlled experiments on soils of varying types are being conducted at the present time. The subject has been brought into prominence as a result of the advent of powerful crawler

9

tractors which make it possible to plough to depths of 18 inches and even more.

There is no question that in some cases the results of deep ploughing have been striking, but not in all; and we are badly in need of more exact information on the subject. One of the difficulties in the past has been to separate the two factors of deep ploughing and high farming, for in nearly all cases where deep ploughing has been adopted, it has been adopted by men who also farm their land intensively in other ways. There is no doubt about the excellence of the crops grown by those who practise deep ploughing, but how much of their success is to be attributed to deep ploughing and how much to high farming it is impossible yet to say.

IF APPLES BLOOM IN MARCH
IN VAIN FOR THEM YOU'LL SEARCH;
IF APPLES BLOOM IN APRIL
WHY THEN THEY'LL BE PLENTIFUL;
IF APPLES BLOOM IN MAY
YOU MAY EAT THEM NIGHT AND DAY

In this country the factor which most often limits the apple crop is spring frost. Clearly the earlier the apple trees blossom the greater the risk of damage by frost.

When old cats play it means rain

Formerly pear trees were of particularly slow growth and many years elapsed before they came into bearing. Hence the couplet:

> 'Plant pears,
> For your heirs.'

But this proverb has lost a great part of its force, since there are now a number of varieties known which yield well in a comparatively short time.

THOUGH DRAINED THE LAND 'TIS CLAY LAND STILL

By reason of their texture it is necessary to drain clay soils if they are to be productive. This is often very costly since the drains on such land must not be too deep and therefore cannot be very far apart. But when the operation is completed, though the productivity of the land will have been greatly increased, yet in texture it will still remain essentially the same as before with all the inherent disadvantages and limitations of clay land. Moreover, however well the drainage has been done it is hopeless from the nature of the case to expect water to percolate through such soil with the same ease and rapidity with which it passes through sands or gravels.

The farther the sight the nearer the rain

This is a saying confined to areas of heavy clay arable land, and in these days of tractors has even more point than before. How often after a few days of drying March wind is the young and inexperienced heavy-land farmer tempted to get ahead with his spring cultivations by rolling his autumn-sown wheats? The roll goes clean, and he is delighted with the progress he is making. But he has forgotten what is happening below the surface; on the top the land may be dry, but it may still be mud inside, and, even if the spring remains a dry one, he will have done more harm than good, and the wheel tracks of the tractor may be visible right up to harvest. If April prove to be wet he will be in a worse mess still, for the water will not be able to penetrate the compressed and puddled clay and will remain lying about in pools on the surface. He is then an April fool indeed. On such land patience is indeed a virtue and the farmer must make haste slowly.

Under *March's Husbandry* Tusser has the following lines:

'If clod in thy wheat, will not break with the frost,
  If now ye do roll it, it quiteth the cost;
  But see when ye roll it, the weather be dry,
  Or else it were better, unrolled to lie.'

When the hen doth moult before the cock,
The winter will be as hard as a rock;
But if the cock moult before the hen
The winter will not wet your shoes' seam

A EWE FULL OF LIFE IS BETTER THAN
ONE FULL OF TEETH

There is grave doubt as to whether this is an ancient saw at all and not just a modern wisecrack. But whether it is old or new it deserves to be recorded, and should be inscribed in letters of gold on the walls of every shepherd's hut. 'Sound in tooth and udder' is the common description of draft ewes exposed for sale. No doubt both are desirable, but how many first-rate breeding ewes have been condemned because they had broken mouths, ewes which were superior in every other respect to many which have been saved because they were sound in the teeth? Sound in the udder they must be, but bodily condition and general vitality are better indicators of a profitable ewe than the state of her mouth.

A SHEEP'S WORST ENEMY IS ANOTHER SHEEP

Nothing is more harmful to successful shepherding than overstocking with sheep. On a farm where a flock of 300 breeding ewes is very profitable, one of 500 may be very unprofitable, and the explanation is the extreme susceptibility of sheep to internal parasites. Much of the ancient technique of sheep husbandry—particularly as it concerns grassland shepherding—is designed to overcome this worm menace. The remarkable way in which for the first two or three years sheep will flourish when they are introduced on to the grassland of a farm which has kept no sheep for many years has to be experienced to be believed. The fortunes which were made when sheep were first introduced on a large scale into the Highlands of Scotland were not due merely to favourable economic circumstances, but to the extraordinary way in which the sheep throve on the clean, unstained ground. The constant change from field to field that lambs demand is another manifestation of the same thing; as another old saw puts it: 'Sheep should never hear the church bells ring twice in the same field.'

We are fortunate these days in knowing a good deal about the life history and habits of these parasites and we are therefore in a much better position to control them; moreover, in recent years certain new drugs have been discovered which are a great advance on anything previously obtainable. But prevention is still better than cure.

THERE ARE MORE BAD FARMERS THAN BAD FARMS

This alas, is true, though it should never be forgotten that bad times are responsible for much bad farming. The law of diminishing returns (the law which states that each increment in the cost of production, whether labour or manure, gives rise to a smaller proportionate return, until a point is reached when the value of the increased yield is more than balanced by the outlay) is not unfortunately just a figment of the economist's imagination, but a law which can be seen in operation in any period of agricultural depression. The level of prices at which it begins to operate is lower in the case of good land than of poor since the costs of production are

14

always less in the case of the former than the latter—hence the saying: 'Good land makes good farmers.' Good land certainly *attracts* good farmers and (though there are brilliant exceptions) the worst are generally found on the poorer farms, which is unfortunate, since it requires more skill and enterprise to farm poor land profitably than good.

A BULL SHOULD BE NOT ONLY ONE OF A GOOD SORT, BUT ALSO A GOOD SORT OF BULL

Until quite recently this would have been better the other way round, putting the emphasis on the bull's breeding rather than on his appearance. There is no doubt that in the past our farmers tended to judge bulls solely upon their appearance. This may be all very well if beef is the only consideration (though it is not ideal even for this), but with bulls of dairy and dual purpose breeds it is clearly entirely inadequate. But in these days the pendulum seems to be swinging to the other extreme; though it is surely just as unwise to judge a bull solely on his breeding, ignoring his appearance, as the reverse. I know that not everyone will agree with me, and we shall all be dead before it can be proved which of us is right. Meanwhile, I think we shall be safe if we stick to the saw.

If there's ice in November that will bear a duck,
There'll be nothing but slush and muck

I frankly do not believe this. I am not sure that I even understand it. It is possible that this is not the original and authentic version. But if it means what it says then the assumption is that a wet week-end at Easter will inevitably be followed by a wet spring and summer in which hay-making will be difficult, though grass will grow luxuriantly. It is true that the phase of the moon at Easter is always the same, and that a great many people believe in weather forecasts based on the state of the weather when the moon is in a certain phase. But I am afraid that an examination of the facts indicates no connection between the weather prevailing at Easter and the weather for the rest of the spring and summer.

There is an alternative rendering which is equally difficult to understand:

> 'A good deal of rain on Easter Day
> Gives crop of good corn but little good hay.'

Plenty of rain about Easter-time may be good for corn, but it is equally good for grass, and since there is no connection between the state of the weather at Easter and its state at the time of hay-making there is no reason to suppose that a good crop of grass will not lead to a good crop of hay.

*A black frost is a long frost, but a white frost never lasts
more than three days*

AN ELDERN STAKE AND WHITETHORN ETHER,
WILL MAKE A HEDGE TO LAST FOR EVER

There is no hedging plant so satisfactory as whitethorn. It has many advantages; it makes a fence capable of holding both sheep and cattle, it is long lived and it grows very few lateral roots, hence the whitethorn ether recommended in the adage.

But if a whitethorn hedge is to be kept from getting hollow at the bottom it will require to be cut and laid from time to time. For this purpose dead stakes are used, and no wood makes better stakes than elder, for elder will last in the ground.

[According to the *Oxford Dictionary* a hedge consists of 'stake' and 'edder' or 'ether', the edder being the bushy part of the hedge woven horizontally in and out of the stakes.]

HE THAT WOULD HAVE HIS FOLD FULL
MUST KEEP AN OLD TUP AND A YOUNG BULL;
HE THAT WOULD HAVE A FULL FLOCK
MUST HAVE AN OLD STAGGE, AND A YOUNG COCK

Young animals are, on the whole, more fertile than old ones, and if this is the only consideration then undoubtedly the adage is right in recommending a young bull and a young cock. A young bull too has the added advantage that it is generally better tempered than an old one, and therefore less dangerous. But fertility is by no means the only consideration in stockbreeding, and in recent years great stress has been laid on the value of the old 'proven' sire, more particularly in the case of dairy bulls. The worth of a dairy bull as a sire remains uncertain until his first dozen daughters complete their first lactations. By this time the bull himself will be an old bull—old, that is, in the sense that he will be above the average age to which bulls in this country are usually kept. If he has been properly managed, however, there is no reason why he should not be as fertile as a young bull, and remain fertile for many more years.

Exactly why an old tup (i.e. ram) should be recommended is not clear. In these days, with the quick maturing Down breeds at least, a ram lamb is generally preferred, though on the whole I am inclined to think that an older sheep is more effective in getting a higher proportion of his ewes in lamb at the first service. Presumably before the characteristic of early maturity had been developed this tendency would be even more marked, and it may well have been that a hundred years ago ram lambs were not effective sires.

A stagge is, I believe, a turkey cock or 'gobbler', and I gather that old turkey cocks are still preferred.

CUCKOO OATS AND WOODCOCK HAY
MAKES THE FARMER RUN AWAY

Oats, if they are to be successful, must in the south at least, be sown early. If they are not sown before the advent of the cuckoo the chances of a good crop are slender.

If the autumn is so wet that the woodcocks arrive before the 'eddish' or second crop hay is saved there is little chance of ever saving it.

'Little and often' is the golden rule for the feeding of all young creatures, and is by no means confined to children and chickens. Because calves which are being reared on the bucket are usually fed only twice a day and never more than three times, they never thrive so well as calves which are running with the cow where they receive their food in a dozen little meals in the course of the twenty-four hours, though the total amount of the milk they so obtain may be no more than that which the bucket-fed calves receive.

HE THAT MARLS SAND

MAY BUY THE LAND.

HE THAT MARLS MOSS

SHALL HAVE NO LOSS.

HE THAT MARLS CLAY

THROWS ALL AWAY

Marl is a mixture of lime and clay, and when added in sufficient quantity to 'sour', 'acid' or lime-deficient sandy soils has the advantage not only of correcting the acidity but improving the texture of the soil as well by giving it cohesion and improving its water-holding capacity. The classic example of marling in this country was the improvement of his Holkam Estate by the great Coke of Norfolk subsequently created Earl of Leicester. Here was a great tract of poor, sour, sandy land, much of it uncultivated, which was transformed in the course of a generation into a prosperous and highly farmed area largely by marling.

Marl, for the same reasons is beneficial when applied to 'moss' (i.e. light, sour, peaty land), but is obviously of no use when applied to a clay soil, since adding clay to clay will not improve its texture, and is an expensive form in which to add lime, even if the clay soil is lime-deficient.

A COW LITTLE GIVETH
THAT HARDLY LIVETH

This is merely a recognition that something cannot be obtained from nothing, though it is amazing how many people fail to recognize the connection between the amount of food a cow receives and the amount of milk that she gives.

Even our best modern dairy cows cannot create matter, and though for a time they may draw upon their own bodily reserves in order to maintain their yield of milk, this cannot continue indefinitely, and ultimately the point is reached when the output of milk exactly corresponds with the intake of nutrients.

FETLOCKS, FEET AND FEATHER;
TOPS MAY COME BUT BOTTOMS NEVER

This rhyme embodies the great truth, that a colt with defective feet and joints can never grow into a valuable horse, no matter how attractive it may be in other ways. Good feet and joints are fundamental, and the plainest, rawest-boned, least attractive youngster with a good set of limbs may, and often will, develop into a first-rate animal at maturity. As another old saying goes: 'Of a ragged colt cometh many a good horse.' Another old saw, familiar to all horsemen, 'No foot, no horse', emphasizes the supreme importance of this part of the animal's anatomy.

COPPER UNDER HEATHER, SILVER UNDER GORSE, GOLD UNDER BRACKEN

The five-year experience of many War Agricultural Committees bears out the truth of this adage exactly. Much heathland was ploughed and cropped, and where the heath was covered with a strong growth of bracken, after it had been well ploughed and well limed, the resulting crops were generally surprisingly good. Where, however, the heathland was of the heathery type the results were generally indifferent, and most Committees soon gave up any attempt to bring such land into cultivation.

The gorse-covered heath seems to be intermediate between the two. It is certainly much more hopeful than heather, but is far more laborious to clear, and when it *is* cleared the results are not as a rule so good as with bracken land.

When sheep rise early to feed, rain is ahead

The difficulty of judging foals is well recognized. Speaking as one who has had considerable experience I should say that there are no classes so difficult to judge as foal classes, and how few foals that win them are ever seen or heard of again! This perhaps explains the saw at least in part.

But there is another reason; the foal stage is generally the most expensive stage at which to buy a horse. To begin with there is the uncertainty of how the foal will develop and the risks that always attach more to colts than to any other class of young stock. Then, too, the most expensive and critical period of the animal's life is still ahead of it—the first winter —when it will be made or marred, according to the treatment it receives. A foal must be really well done at this time if it is ever to make a valuable horse. Yet in spite of all this the price of a yearling in the spring or summer is little more than the price of the same animal as a foal the previous autumn. It is difficult to explain this. Certainly a foal is always an attractive little beast, whereas a yearling is at a very ugly stage in its development, and is inclined to be all legs and wings. A foal is always something of a gamble and that is perhaps one of its chief attractions!

Evening grey and morning red,
Sends the shepherd wet to bed.
Evening red and morning grey
Is the sign of a very fine day

SOW FOUR GRAINS IN A ROW,
ONE FOR THE PIGEON, ONE FOR THE CROW,
ONE TO ROT AND ONE TO GROW

Are we to assume from this that only one-quarter of the grain sown will become plants? At first sight this may seem to be rather a pessimistic estimate, though as a matter of fact in the days when the adage originated it may well have been an understatement. As a result of many careful investigations we know pretty accurately the position to-day, that from 70 to 85 per cent of the seed we sow actually give plants, of which about 70 per cent survive until harvest; in other words, rather less than one-half of the grain that we sow to-day is wasted, a result nearly twice as good as the adage suggests.

When we compare to-day's conditions with those that prevailed a hundred years ago, and still more if we compare them with those of the Middle Ages, the difference is explained. To-day good seed, clean and of high germinating capacity, is always obtainable; the seed is drilled at a uniform depth into a well-prepared seed-bed and is all covered. A hundred years ago, good seed was not always obtainable; it was broadcast on the surface, and though it was harrowed in, the loss from birds must have been considerable.

It is interesting to note that the pigeon is specifically mentioned as being responsible for a large part of the loss, not the obvious bird that we should think of in this connection to-day. Yet in medieval times it must have been a perfect scourge, though it was the domestic pigeon and not the wild pigeon that was the chief culprit.

Mr H. S. Bennett in his book, *Life on the English Manor*, writes: 'Another nuisance to the peasant was the dove or pigeon. The lord's dove-house was one of the most familiar of medieval sights. No peasant was allowed to have one, or to kill these birds, however numerous they were, and however harmful to his crops. Large dove-houses, sometimes holding hundreds of birds, were built, and from thence hordes of these voracious feeders descended on the unfortunate peasant's fields, taking their fill, and fattening themselves for the lord's table at his men's expense. Little wonder that the dove-house became one of the most hated landmarks of the lord's position and of the subjection of the villagers.'

To-day where a crop of wheat sustains much bird damage, as it often may when it is sown late, the chief culprit is usually the starling, a bird which we know to have increased enormously in numbers of late years and which has apparently changed its habits as a result.

A SWARM OF BEES IN MAY
IS WORTH A LOAD OF HAY.
A SWARM OF BEES IN JUNE
IS WORTH A SILVER SPOON.
BUT A SWARM OF BEES IN JULY
ISN'T WORTH A FLY

It is obvious that an early swarm of bees is more valuable than a late one, but why, except that *load of hay* rhymes with May and *silver spoon* rhymes with June, these are taken as standards

of value it is impossible to guess. Tusser values an early swarm
of bees at a crown (which in the sixteenth century was a
goodly sum, probably much more than the value of a load of
hay), for under *May's Husbandry* he says:

> 'Take heed to thy bees, that are ready to swarm,
> The loss thereof now is a crown's worth of harm;
> Let skilful be ready, and diligence seen,
> Lest being too careless, thou losest thy been.'

WHEN THE WIND IS IN THE NORTH
THE SKILFUL FISHER GOES NOT FORTH.
WHEN THE WIND IS IN THE SOUTH
IT BLOWS THE BAIT IN THE FISH'S MOUTH.
WHEN THE WIND IS IN THE EAST
THEY WON'T BITE IN THE LEAST.
BUT WHEN THE WIND IS IN THE WEST
THE FISH BITE BEST

No doubt these lines are true in the main, though most
anglers worth the name could and would tell of many exceptions: as, for instance, when conditions seemed perfect and
yet not a fish would feed; or when conditions were anything
but propitious and yet good sport was obtained. This, however,
is all part of the glorious uncertainty of angling, and (a friend
adds) of the indomitable loquacity of anglers among themselves.

A good hearing day is a sign of wet

Cattle at grass begin to feel the pinch of winter toward the end of November. Unless the season is an unusually open one and there is still plenty of rough pulling on the pastures, they will then begin to go back in condition. It is sound practice to prevent this when possible either by bringing them inside, or by supplementing their pasture with hay and straw. If this is not done early in order to prevent loss of condition it will have to be done later if the weakest cattle are not to perish; for from Christmas onwards cattle, which have been falling in condition (supplementing their scanty rations off their own backs as it were), will reach a point when, having exhausted their own resources, they will literally starve, though the process of starvation may be slow. It will be the weakest cattle, those in poorest condition to start with, and which therefore had the smallest resources to draw upon, which will 'decay' most. Up to 150 years ago it was impossible to prevent cattle from shrinking to skin and bone during the winter, and the losses among them must have been heavy indeed. The risk of 'hoven' to such cattle when the grass grew in the spring can well be understood. Tusser summed up the position in his verse:

> 'From Christmas till May be well entered in,
>   Some cattle wax faint, and look poorly and thin;
>   And chiefly when prime grass at first doth appear,
>   Then most is the danger of all the whole year.'

This is undoubtedly true of the influence that the bull exerts upon the character of the calves that are born in the herd. Every calf owes as much to its sire as to its dam. Some people believe that the influence of the sire in respect of the milking qualities of his daughters is greater than that of the dam, but there is no evidence to support this, and it is now generally accepted that the influences of both are equal. But since the bull will be the sire of all the calves born in the herd, whereas each cow will produce only one each year, it is clear that in this respect he is half the herd.

It is by means of the bull that a herd can most easily be improved, and it is surprising how a herd of very moderate cows can be transformed in the course of two or three generations by the use of superior bulls. This 'grading up' of herds by using a succession of good pedigree bulls of the same breed is very much to be encouraged. Most breeds with 'open' herdbooks require four top crosses of pedigree sires before the female progeny are given full pedigree status, and five top crosses in the case of males, which mean that thirty-one out of its thirty-two great-great-grandparents were pedigree animals.

If the ash before the oak
Then we'll surely have a soak,
If the oak before the ash
Then we'll only have a splash

This presumably refers to spring sowing, for in autumn, particularly in some seasons, much wheat has to be sown when the land is wet if it is to be sown at all, and what is more, appears to suffer little harm as a result. Spring sowing, however, is a very different matter, and with a crop like barley it is imperative to wait until conditions are favourable before sowing is attempted.

It is possible, however, that the adage refers to the sowing on ill-drained and water-logged land generally. If so it is a hundred per cent right for it is always folly to attempt to grow crops on such land, at best they will be poor and often they will fail completely. 'Drainage is the first of all improvements' is another good old saying. To spend money on liming and manuring water-logged land is waste, for nothing will effect any real improvement until it has first been drained.

NEVER OFFER YOUR HEN FOR SALE ON A RAINY DAY

The way in which stock are presented for sale makes a tremendous difference to the prices they fetch. Perhaps this should not be so, but that it is so nobody will deny. The best hen in the world would be a miserable-looking object on a wet day, and her appearance then will certainly not commend her to a prospective purchaser.

There is a saying to the effect that 'nothing sells so well as condition', and it is true that an animal that carries a certain amount of flesh will look so much better than another of the same sort in poor condition, that it will command a very much higher price, a difference out of all proportion to the cost of the additional food that it has consumed.

Cattle-dealers and horse-dealers, as would be expected, are masters in the art of presenting animals for sale in attractive condition. This of course is part of their business. Cattle and sheep whose stomachs are full look far better than those whose stomachs are empty, and beasts which can be marketed with the 'bloom' on them, coming direct from field to market without a long journey, always look pounds better.

In my experience cattle at grass never look so well as they do in the evening when the shadows are long. This is undoubtedly the best time to show them to a prospective purchaser!

ALL GOES TO THE DEVIL,
WHERE SHEPHERD IS EVIL

It is not so many years ago since the majority of our large *arable* farms were dominated by the needs of the ewe flock. On such farms the shepherds were complete autocrats, and ruled with a rod of iron. It was generally a benevolent tyranny, but, where it was not the whole farm suffered.

Mr A. G. Street in *Farmer's Glory* draws a vivid picture of such a farm, and it is by no means overdrawn. The tyranny of the shepherd has to be experienced to be believed.

But since this adage dates from before the introduction of the root crop into British farming, it cannot refer to arable sheep flocks and their shepherds. Its purpose is probably to emphasize the dominating influence of the shepherd upon the well-being of his flock. No one who has ever been responsible for managing a flock of ewes is likely to underestimate the importance of the shepherd. Good shepherds are born and not made. By education and training a good shepherd can no doubt be improved, but no amount of teaching and experience will make a bad shepherd good.

Shepherding runs in families and the best shepherds are generally the sons and grandsons of shepherds. A good shepherd seems to know by instinct what will suit his flock, and their reaction to any proposed change. He is able, as it were, to think like a sheep. Shepherding is still largely an art and demands the right temperament, a quick eye, devotion to duty and a passion for sheep. When the shepherd is endowed with these qualities the flock will flourish; where they are absent the flock will fail. There is an old saying to the effect that no man is fit to be a flockmaster who cannot sit on a hurdle and look at a sheep for an hour. If this be true of the flockmaster it is not less true of the shepherd.

A DRY AND FROSTY JANIVEER
IS LIKE TO MAKE A PLENTEOUS YEAR

There are several rhymes which emphasize the advantages of seasonable weather in January, and the disadvantages of unseasonable weather. Cold, dry, frosty weather at this time of the year will do a minimum of harm and a maximum of good.

The only harm it can possibly do is to autumn-sown beans, and some varieties of winter oats, for, unlike wheat, beans and winter oats are not absolutely winter hardy and in a severe frost may suffer considerably—particularly if it be a wind frost. But the good that a month of hard frost can do to the texture of the soil is immense, and as a result of it ideal seed beds will be obtained for spring sowing with a minimum of effort. A mild (and particularly a wet) January is always disliked. Everything starts growing prematurely only to be cut back by the subsequent return of cold weather:

> 'A January spring,
> Is worth nothing.'

Or, according to another rhyme on the same theme:

> 'If you see grass in January
> Lock your grain in your granary.'

FIVE EWES ALLOW
TO EVERY COW

This couplet remains unchanged since the time of Tusser, though as used to-day its meaning is entirely different. By it Tusser meant that five ewes gave as much milk as a cow. If he was right, then either our cows to-day are very much better milkers than those of his time or our ewes are much inferior in this respect—probably the former.

When quoted to-day it generally refers to the comparative amounts of food required by sheep and cattle. In this connection it is inaccurate, for though five *small* ewes suckling *single* lambs require approximately as much food as one cow giving two gallons of milk a day, yet three large ewes suckling twins will require as much. Alternatively it is sometimes used to indicate the supposed correct ratio of sheep to cattle in mixed grazing. In this connection too it is inaccurate except perhaps on hill grazings, for on good grassland five sheep to one cow would be considered too many. Most farmers would prefer a ratio of not more than three to every beast.

A FARMER SHOULD LIVE AS THOUGH HE WERE GOING
   TO DIE TO-MORROW,
BUT HE SHOULD FARM AS THOUGH HE WERE GOING
   TO LIVE FOR EVER

It is unnecessary to comment on the first part of this saw which is obviously true and is not confined to farmers. The second part is no less true, though perhaps less obvious.

A successful farmer may be defined as one who farms profitably, but not at the expense either of his employees or his farm. In other words, no farmer can be called successful who does not maintain the fertility of his land. To do this means the adoption of a long-term policy; hand to mouth methods will not suffice. A good farmer must always plan ahead—often years ahead. He must be far-sighted, and take long views. He cannot, for example, hope to see any return on the money which he spends to-day on the purchase of an expensive dairy bull, until that bull's daughters themselves come into the dairy in four years' time. He spends money in draining a field knowing well that it will be some years before he gets his money back. No farmer who farms simply for the current year without care or thought for the succeeding years can claim to be a good farmer.

IN THE SPRING, HAIR IS WORTH MORE THAN MEAT

The reference here is to the fact that out-wintered store cattle (which therefore carry heavy coats in the spring) are very much more valuable than cattle that have been wintered inside in comparatively warm yards and, as a result, have no winter coats, though they will very probably carry more flesh. The out-wintered cattle will start to 'do' and to put on weight as soon as ever the grass begins to grow in the spring, while those that have been wintered inside will, as the result of chills and scouring, inevitably 'go back' for the first month after they are turned out to grass. In consequence, in the spring out-wintered store cattle are at a premium.

LIME AND LIME WITHOUT MANURE
MAKES THE FARM AND FARMER POOR

It is difficult to-day to imagine any farmer repeatedly spending good money on liming his land without at the same time manuring it. But if we are to believe the adage, some farmers must at some time have needed the warning. It is, however, only necessary to substitute (if the laws of metre would allow it) the words *sulphate of ammonia* for *lime* and the adage is immediately brought up to date and deserves another long lease of life!

WHEAT EVER—BARLEY NEVER

Here we must tread warily, for we are on dangerous ground. The adage refers to the almost universal practice among farmers of changing their seed wheat—in some cases every year—a practice which the proverb commends, while condemning a similar practice with seed barley. Any tradition that is widely held among farmers, as this one is, demands the greatest respect, and cannot be treated lightly. The practice is certainly old; Tusser is referring to it when he says:

'Good neighbours indeed
Change seed for seed.'

Yet a good deal of experimental work has been done to test the advantage of changing seed wheat from one soil to another and from one district to another, without any measurable benefit having been observed. If the farmer's own seed wheat is a good and well-ripened sample, true to variety, clean, and with a high germinating capacity, there seems nothing gained in changing it for seed wheat grown on some other type of soil or in some other district. Sanders in his *Outline of British Crop Husbandry* says: 'It is clearly unwise to be dogmatic in the face of so much practical opinion, but the probabilities are not in favour of any advantages being gained from changing seed, except where that is the only method of obtaining a sample which is well ripened and free from disease.'

It seems possible that the last phrase gives the clue to the origin of the tradition. *Covered Smut* or *Bunt* is a seed-borne disease of wheat; it was the curse of our forefathers and they did not know how to control it. Hence frequent change of seed may have been necessary. To-day we know how to control it; and all worthy farmers, before sowing their seed wheat, dress it either with formalin, copper sulphate, or one of the newer mercurial seed-dressings. If this was the reason for changing seed wheat, the reason has disappeared. But the tradition still persists.

Moreover, we may well ask if 'Wheat ever' why 'Barley never'? Possibly the answer is that as barley does not suffer from *Bunt* like wheat, there was never the same reason for changing the seed. In addition there is a strong argument in favour of continually growing the same stock of barley on the same farm. As Sanders puts it: 'If a stock of seed is introduced, those plants which are most suited will thrive best and will, therefore, contribute more than their quota to the bulk of seed obtained; thus if the stock be grown for several years there will be a constant natural selection from it of the physiological strains most successful in the given conditions. In support might be quoted the fact that if spring oats are sown in autumn, though mortality is very high, the surviving strains may display a marked increase in winter hardiness over the original bulk. It is possible therefore, on purely theoretical grounds, to argue against change of seed.'

Many large arable land sheep farms on the chalk include an area of 'down', which has been used as a sheep-walk from time immemorial. The ewes are folded on the arable land, but are given a run out every day on to the down. Since the grassland has always been grazed heavily, and often exclusively, by sheep, it naturally is infested with all the worms to which sheep are a prey. It is, however, alleged that, if the ewes are not taken on to these infected grounds until the dew is off and the grass is dry, they stand little chance of becoming infected, for when the sun gets up (and the dew disappears) the worm goes down.

TO BREAK A PASTURE MAKES A MAN
TO MAKE A PASTURE BREAKS A MAN

It is hardly an exaggeration to say that the first line of this adage has formed the basis of the Government's war-time agricultural policy. The fertility stored up in well-managed grassland has been utilized to good purpose during these last few years, and under the plough such fields have yielded splendid crops of wheat, oats, and potatoes, which have been of the greatest value at a critical time. The knowledge that old grassland is a rich storehouse of plant food, which can best be turned to account by ploughing, is by no means new. That it was not put into practice to any degree in pre-war years was due in part to the general unprofitableness of arable

farming, and in part to belief in the second half of the adage, a belief which is without justification. There is no doubt, however, that up to fifty years ago the making of a permanent pasture was a dark and difficult adventure, and one not to be undertaken lightly. At best it was a slow and expensive business, and even in the most favoured districts the results were uncertain.

Not so to-day, however, and the difference is not so much due to our increased skill and knowledge as to the fact that now we have at our disposal certain things which were denied our ancestors—things which make the whole difference between success and failure. In the absence of a proper supply of grass seed, of wild white clover seed, and of phosphates, who would undertake the putting down of a field to permanent grass with any degree of confidence? Yet this is what our great-grandfathers had to do; small wonder that they regarded it with dismay, and that their justifiable fears and trepidations should have outlived them.

A LATE SPRING NEVER DECEIVES

Though a late spring has certain disadvantages, particularly for those who are trying to winter a big head of stock on a limited quantity of hay and straw, it is never disastrous in its effects. Grass in a late spring may be postponed by three weeks or more, and this is extremely inconvenient, but is not to be compared to the damage suffered by fruit-growers when a burst of abnormally early spring weather brings out all the blossom, only to be cut by a return of wintry conditions later. In such seasons the entire crop may be destroyed and the work of a whole year lost overnight. This is when an early spring deceives, a thing a late one can never do.

There is a chance that in the not-too-distant future fruit-growers may be able to overcome the ill-effects of an early burst of spring weather by spraying their trees with preparations (now under experiment) designed to delay blossoming in such circumstances. If these experiments are successful a great deal of the hazard connected with fruit-growing will be removed.

SUMMER IN WINTER AND A SUMMER FLOOD NEVER BODED ENGLAND GOOD

The ideal sequence is a dry and frosty winter followed by a showery spring and a sunny and comparatively dry summer. A mild open winter is bad, a wet summer is worse, but a combination of the two is disastrous.

THE FROST HURTS NO WEEDS

This does not mean that all weeds are winter-hardy, though most perennial weeds are. But frost will not hurt the annual weeds in the sense that it will reduce their number the following year, for long before they are killed by frost they will have seeded and the damage will have been done.

If an arable field is flooded for any length of time during the winter it will not produce a good crop that year. Of course, if the field was sown with winter wheat the crop will probably be killed outright, nor will it grow a satisfactory spring-sown crop subsequently. It is stagnant water that does so much harm.

Snow, however, is often beneficial, for it may save a crop from serious damage by wind frosts. A field of beans (a crop which is not completely winter-hardy) under snow will suffer no harm however severe the weather, so long as it remains covered.

WHO IN JANUARY SOWS OATS
GETS GOLD AND GROATS;
WHO SOWS IN MAY
GETS LITTLE THAT WAY

One of the most serious pests of spring-sown oats in southern England is the frit fly. The first attack begins about the end of April and continues until the middle of June. The susceptibility of the plant to attack is most marked during the two-leaf and three-leaf stages of growth; beyond the four-leaf stage susceptibility decreases very rapidly. If oats are sown early and have passed this stage in their development by the time that the frit flies first swarm, they will escape injury. Hence the desirability of early sowing (provided, of course, that soil conditions are favourable).

43

The annual loss caused by this minute fly in England alone is very great, and before the war was estimated at two million pounds sterling; half of this loss is due to the first spring attack, which can be avoided only by having the oat plants past the susceptible stage by the time it occurs.

IF IN FEBRUARY THERE BE NO RAIN
'TIS NEITHER GOOD FOR HAY NOR GRAIN

A dry February is unusual; but though I have heard many complaints of excessive wet in February I have never yet heard a farmer complain of this month that it has been too dry.

IT IS ONLY VERY YOUNG CLAY-LAND FARMERS
WHO EVER WISH FOR RAIN

I well remember years ago receiving this reproof from an old and experienced clay-land farmer, and I have often thought since how right he was.

It was when I complained one autumn of my land being so hard and dry that I couldn't drill my wheat. A wet summer had been followed by a hot and dry autumn. My land, which was clay, had been ploughed after harvest when it was rather wet, and, as a result of the dry autumn, had set into blocks as hard as concrete. It required heavy rain to soften them. The rain came of course in time, and continued as though it would never stop. I have never complained of dry weather since, though in company with other clay-land farmers I continually complain of too much rain—and have never been rebuked for it!

LEAP YEAR WAS NE'ER A GOOD SHEEP YEAR

This is sheer superstition. All the fact it has in it is that 'sheep' rhymes with 'leap'.

SHEAR YOUR SHEEP IN MAY
AND YOU'LL SHEAR THEM ALL AWAY

Obviously the date of shearing varies in different parts of the country. There is, however, a universal temptation to shear early, not so much because the weight of wool will be greater as because of the increased risk of 'fly' among unshorn sheep and the greater difficulty of dealing with them when they are struck. By an early spell of hot weather inexperienced flockmasters are sometimes tempted to shear early, with very detrimental results to their sheep should the weather revert to wet and cold. As another old saying puts it: 'Who shears his sheep before St Gervatin's Day, loves more his wool than his sheep.'

WHEN THE SAND DOTH FEED THE CLAY,
ENGLAND WOE, AND WELL-A-DAY;
BUT WHEN THE CLAY DOTH FEED THE SAND
THEN 'TIS WELL FOR ENGLE-LAND

I am not sure of the meaning of this rhyme; I think it must mean that agriculture in England flourishes only when wheat-growing is profitable. For wheat is really the only directly cashable crop that can be grown on clay land, and if wheat

45

cannot be grown profitably then such land is no longer worth ploughing. But on the lighter classes of land good malting barley may be grown, which may still be very saleable even though the price of wheat is low. In other words, it is a poor prospect for England when it is profitable to farm light land but not heavy. We certainly had a clear example of this between the two wars, when many clay-land farmers went bankrupt, and much clay land went out of cultivation, because the price of wheat was so low; though light-land farmers were still able to carry on with the help of barley and sugar-beet.

CHANGE OF PASTURE MAKES FAT CALVES

A benefit from change of pasture is by no means confined to calves; it applies even more to lambs, and indeed to all classes of stock. There are advantages, too, to the pasture itself. The modern technique of 'on and off' grazing emphasizes this point. Efficient grazing does not consist of just putting so many head of stock into a field, shutting the gate and leaving them there for the whole summer; though this practice is all too common. As the growth of grass is not equal throughout the summer, such a system must mean that the pasture is either hopelessly undergrazed during certain periods of the year or badly overgrazed at others, and both undergrazing and overgrazing are very damaging to good swards.

It is interesting to observe how greedily cattle and sheep will graze a fresh pasture into which they have been newly

46

moved, even though there was still plenty of grass on the one which they have just vacated. Presumably no two pastures are identical, certainly no two old pastures, and it is possible that the stock may get from one what they are unable to get from another. One of the complaints most constantly made about leys is that they are too uniformly alike, and it is certainly true that stock will do better on young leys if they are changed back on to old pasture at intervals.

IF YOUR FARM IS MANNED WITH BOYS AND HORSED WITH COLTS, YOUR FOOD IS ALL EATEN AND YOUR WORK UNDONE

This is a tribute to the value of experience. There is an old saying to the effect that if you employ one boy you will have one boy to work for you, if you employ two boys you will have only half a boy, and if you employ three you won't have a boy at all. If you are foolish enough to put all your boys to work together this will very likely be true.

To have no horses except colts would be equally unfortunate; you would have no shaft horses, and no experienced horses for horse-hoeing and similar tasks, where a horse must know how to walk a row. I can well believe that a combination of boys and colts would be disastrous.

When a toad crosses the road on a summer afternoon,
rain is at hand

IF THE MOON IS FULL AT CHRISTMAS NO BLACK
FLY WILL BE SEEN ON THE BEANS

The attacks of black aphis, which often do serious damage to the bean crop, are far worse in some years than in others, but there is of course no connection between the severity of the attack and the phase of the moon at Christmas.

A very good indication, however, of the severity of the attack to be expected the following summer may be obtained by examining spindle trees during the winter. The black fly lays its eggs on these trees at the end of the summer, and it is the eggs which form the overwintering stage of this pest. A close examination of shoots and buds of spindle trees during the winter may reveal a large number of black aphis eggs, which are black shining objects, rather smaller in size than a pin's head. By making counts of the numbers of eggs present on spindle trees entomologists can now predict fairly accurately whether there is likely to be a severe attack of bean aphis in any one district.

HE WHO WOULD GLEAN MUST LEARN TO BEND

This is a little-known proverb, but pleasant. I include it with the excuse that the metaphor is agricultural.

If rain is coming geese always gaggle on the pond

48

Up to the early years of the present century rent figured largely in a farmer's calculations. In those days it was by far the largest single item in his expenditure and dwarfed all the others. It was because of this that, in the depression of the nineties, landlords were able to save their tenants from failure simply by remissions of rent. It is no exaggeration to say that during those years British agriculture was saved from complete disaster by this action of landlords, though it may be argued that they had no alternative, since it is impossible to get blood out of a stone, and if the sitting tenants failed there was then no prospect of replacing them with others.

In the depression between the two wars, rent had ceased to be the outstanding item in the farmer's expenditure—it was just a drop in the ocean; and even had landlords in those days been able to afford to remit their entire rents (which they certainly were not), the remission would not have sufficed to save the situation. In such circumstances, although it was true enough that, plough or plough not, the rent still had to be paid, yet not to plough was the cheapest way out; for, with wheat at £1 a quarter and labour at 30s. a week, less money was lost by not cultivating the land than by cropping it, for even a good crop was so unprofitable that it involved the loss of a sum greater than the rent.

Before rain moles throw up the earth more than usual

A farmer's team may be replenished in three ways; he may breed a sufficient number of foals to provide the necessary replacements, he may buy unbroken youngsters either as foals, yearlings or two-year-olds, or he may rely on buying old or unsound horses which, though unsuitable for road-work, may still be capable of working on the land. What a farmer cannot afford to do in normal times is to replenish his team by purchasing good, sound, quiet five- or six-year-olds, for these are the horses which are suitable for town-work and few farmers can afford to compete with town buyers.

It therefore follows that unless a farmer who relies upon purchasing his requirements, purchase them as colts, he will be reduced to buying unsound or aged animals, in which case he will never have a team worthy of the name.

With skilled labour scarce it becomes more and more difficult to get men capable of breaking and handling colts; in consequence, there was never a greater discrepancy than there is to-day between the price of young unbroken horses and that of broken ones; the former are relatively cheap and the latter often very dear.

St Swithin's day, if thou dost rain,
For forty days it will remain;
St Swithin's day, if thou be fine,
For forty days the sun will shine

GO NORTH WHEN YOUR NEIGHBOURS
ARE ALL GOING SOUTH

There is a great deal of common sense in this piece of advice. For one thing it is generally unwise to start any particular enterprise during a boom period, for this means getting in at a time when prices are high with the prospect of having ultimately to face heavy depreciation. For another thing, it only requires a very small surplus of any commodity to bring its price down to a level out of all proportion to the size of the surplus. Before the days of the Potato Marketing Board there was always a marked tendency for the acreage of potatoes to increase after a year in which potatoes had proved a profitable crop, and two consecutive profitable years were invariably followed by a slump.

DOWN CORN—UP HORN

The assumption here is that when corn growing is unprofitable then large areas of land will be put down to grass, and the cattle population correspondingly increased. It is true enough that large areas are put down to grass when ploughing ceases to be profitable, but it does not follow that the cattle population will rise proportionately—indeed, the cattle population may decline, for the limiting factor to the number of cattle which we can support in this country is winter keep, and not summer keep; and it is the arable land which supplies the bulk of our winter keep. During the six war-years we ploughed up some six million acres of grass and reduced our importations of animal feeding stuffs to a mere fraction of their pre-war quantity, yet our cattle population increased.

NO HORN—NO CORN

This raises the difficult question, whether soil fertility can be maintained without farmyard manure. It is certain that it could not be years ago; in those days the absence of stock inevitably led to a decrease in fertility, and to correspondingly low yields of corn. It used to be the farm that kept the most stock that grew the most corn.

It is still early days to dogmatize on whether it is possible to maintain fertility in these times without stock; for enough stockless farms have not yet been functioning for a sufficient length of time. But I am rather reluctantly coming to the conclusion that it *is* possible on a great many soils, though not on all. But to say that it is *possible* to maintain fertility without farmyard manure is not to say that without it fertility would *probably* be maintained, for I do not think for a moment that it would, and in consequence I think that to advocate any general adoption of stockless farming would be exceedingly dangerous. While some very able farmers, highly mechanized and farming on a large scale, may be able to maintain fertility indefinitely without farmyard manure (N.B. I say *may*), I certainly do not think the average farmer either could or would. Moreover, I doubt if, in the absence of stock, fertility can ever be maintained at the highest level.

HE THAT HATH A GOOD HARVEST MAY BE
CONTENT WITH SOME THISTLES

This is the agricultural version of the proverb 'No rose without a thorn'. Thistles are difficult weeds to control and a farm which is relatively clean may still grow some. Vigorous and strong growing thistles are an indication of good land, and land which will grow a good thistle will also grow good corn. But however good his harvest no farmer is really content, nor should he be. There are always weak places on every farm, even in the best years, often the results of mistakes which the good farmer is the first to acknowledge and which he will resolve not to repeat. It is one of the hardest facts of farming that a farmer's opportunities of profiting by his experience and correcting his mistakes are so limited, for after all very few farmers live long enough to grow fifty harvests.

WHEN YOU'VE DONE WEIGHING YOU'VE
DONE PAYING

This is a reminder that quantity is often more profitable than quality. There is no question that under the Ministry of Food's present regulations of paying for livestock this is true to-day, when the same price per cwt. is paid for a prime two-year-old Aberdeen Angus steer weighing 10 cwt., as for a well-finished but bony four-year-old Friesian steer weighing 16 cwt. But in peace-time the reminder was often necessary that quantity cannot always profitably be sacrificed for the sake of quality. There was never a greater fallacy than to suppose (as the pre-war critics of our farmers always seemed to suppose) that the highest-priced article was necessarily the most profitable to produce. It certainly is not so in industry. Why then should it be so in agriculture? Because the 'Little London' pig slaughtered at four months old was worth several pence per lb. more than a bacon pig weighing 220 lb., it does not necessarily follow that it was the more profitable type of pig to produce, nor was 'baby beef' (a beast weighing 8 cwt. at 16–18 months, the result of expensive forcing from birth) necessarily more profitable (or even as profitable) to produce than a beast that weighed 12 cwt. at $2\frac{1}{2}$ years old, even though the price per cwt. of the former was considerably greater than that of the latter.

WELL SOWN IS HALF GROWN

This is obviously the agricultural version of the proverb 'Well begun is half done', and it is certainly true that the battle for a crop is half won when the seed has been sown with faith and hope in good time and in a perfect seed-bed, for a really good crop will result only from a good 'plant', and a perfect 'plant' demands perfect conditions at the time of sowing. There is a school of thought (which may be described as the 'no cultivation school') which maintains that so long as there is enough tilth to cover the seed nothing else matters, though they always postulate clean land. (Exactly how land is to be kept clean if it is not well cultivated we are not told.)

Given clean land in a high state of fertility they are probably right. Certainly if land is clean and in good heart the conditions at sowing are far less important, though even with such land a good seed-bed is surely an advantage. But a perfect seed-bed depends more upon the timing of the tillage operations than upon their number, and is usually the result of a comparatively few which are well-timed.

I have always thought that the perfect answer to those who were inclined to be persuaded by the arguments of the 'no cultivation school' is to be found in the Book of Proverbs, chapter 28, verse 19: 'He that tilleth his land shall have plenty of bread: but he that followeth after vain persons shall have poverty enough.'

CUT A THISTLE IN MAY
IT WILL GROW NEXT DAY;
CUT IT IN JUNE
IT WILL GROW AGAIN SOON;
CUT IN JULY
IT WILL SURELY DIE;
CUT IN AUGUST
AND DIE IT MUST

I wish that I were as certain that the last four lines of the adage were as true as the first four! Certainly the only chance of killing a thistle by cutting (and it is no more than a chance) is to cut it at a stage when the stores of food in its root stock are exhausted and before it has had time to replenish them. It should then be cut as low as possible, well below the bottom leaves, so that the plant is completely defoliated. A machine can rarely be set to cut low enough, and this is partly why a scythe is more effective for cutting thistles. More effective still is a spud which cuts the thistle below the surface, and most effective of all are the thistle tongs by which the thistle is pulled out root and all. Unfortunately, unless the thistles are very few in number, neither spudding nor pulling is practicable, so that we are reduced to cutting by machine. By cutting at the psychological moment the thistles can be very much weakened, but they will rarely be killed, unless the cutting is repeated and repeated.

ON A FARM WHERE THERE ARE GEESE, THE FARMER'S WIFE WEARS THE BREECHES

Traditionally the poultry on a farm are the perquisite of the farmer's wife. This is perhaps one of the reasons why on so many farms they receive such scant attention from the farmer. Certain it is that no class of poultry is popular with the majority of farmers, and geese are the least popular of all, so much so that in ordinary times few farmers will tolerate their presence. For this they have reason, as geese eat an incredible amount of grass, and compete directly with both sheep and cattle. It has been estimated that seven geese eat as much grass as a cow, and those who have had most experience with geese are the least likely to quarrel with this figure. Moreover, it is not only the amount of grass that geese eat that makes them unpopular but the amount they foul.

56

This is a reference to the belief that if wheat is slow in germinating the ears of the resultant crop will be unusually large. This may very well be the case, for slow germination generally results in a thin 'plant', and the average size of the ear with a thin plant is greater than with a full, the result of reduced competition for light, air, moisture and plant food. It should be noted, however, that a comparatively small number of large ears will not compensate for a large number of smaller ears. In other words, the yield per acre from a thin plant will be less than that from a full, in spite of the fact that the average size of the ears will be greater in the former case than in the latter. But in all cases there is an optimum plant population, the optimum varying with different soils; for example, more plants are required on light, chalky soil than on heavy clay.

A GALLON OF MILK FROM THE COW IS WORTH TWO FROM THE BUCKET

This saw of course refers to calf-rearing, and its truth is generally admitted. Nature never intended the calf to obtain its nourishment other than direct from its own mother, and the nearer natural rearing methods are approached the better the results that will be obtained. Everyone will agree that of all the systems of calf-rearing none is so satisfactory as suckling, for under this system the calves suffer fewer set-backs and thrive and grow more quickly; moreover, this method has the advantage of being practically foolproof. Milk drawn by the calf direct from the udder is clean, it is at the correct temperature, and, as it is consumed only in small mouthfuls instead of in gulps (inevitable in bucket feeding) it is more easily digested. Of course the method is hopelessly expensive if only one calf is suckled per cow, but a good cow can bring up from seven to ten calves in the course of a lactation, generally in three batches, each calf being suckled for three months, starting with three or four calves and finishing with one or two.

THE MAN WHO WALKS TO MARKET LIVES LONGER
THAN THE MAN WHO RIDES

The assumption years ago was that a man who walked to market, walked because he was driving fat stock, whereas the man who rode was delivering corn. There was no question as to which of the two products was the more exhausting to the land. It was the boast of many old farmers that everything they produced walked off their farms. But times have changed, and farmyard manure is not to-day the only form of manure available. It does not follow, however, that it should be neglected, and it is as great a mistake to ignore it as it is to rely solely upon it.

The best farming practice to-day utilizes farmyard manure to the full, and supports it with artificials. In this way heavy crops are secured and the fertility of the soil is maintained. The 'Health and Humus' or the 'Muck and Mystery' school

spoil a very good case by their extravagant claims, and have done a great disservice by condemning all chemical fertilizers. In order to extol the virtues of farmyard manure and compost it is neither necessary nor wise to condemn all artificial manures.

A LOAD OF HAY IN JUNE IS WORTH TWO IN JULY

Young grass has a much higher feeding value than old grass, and this difference remains when it is made into hay. Hay cut in June, when the grass is still young and leafy and when the protein content is high, is far more valuable as a feeding stuff than hay cut in July, by which time the grass has become old, woody and fibrous. It is true that there will be less weight per acre when the hay is cut in June, though the total amount of digestible food obtained will not be diminished. It will, however, be contained within a smaller bulk. It is high time that farmers learned to think, when considering the crops that they grow for the consumption of their own stock, in terms of digestible food per acre rather than to think simply in terms of total bulk.

A rainbow at morn
Put your hook in the corn
A rainbow at eve
Put your head in the sheave

This is just another way of saying that mangolds cannot compete with weeds, and that if a good crop is to be secured it must be kept clean by continued hoeing. Mangolds are sometimes spoken of as a cleaning crop. So no doubt they are if properly managed, but if they are neglected they can be just the reverse. The term 'cleaning crop' is an unfortunate one. It is too often assumed that such a crop, by some peculiar virtue of its own, will clean the land upon which it is grown, whereas it is a cleaning crop only in the sense that owing to the way in which it is grown it provides *opportunities* for cleaning the land. If these opportunities are not taken advantage of such a crop will leave the land very much dirtier than it was before, in fact dirtier than a corn crop would have done if grown in its place.

WHEAT IN MORTAR, BARLEY IN DUST

That winter wheat may be successfully sown under adverse conditions is well known. In fact there is an adage to that effect: 'Sow in a slop—sure of a crop.' The expressions 'treading it in' or 'mauling it in' are sometimes heard in connection with wheat-sowing in a wet autumn on clay land, expressions which it would be unthinkable to use in connection with the sowing of barley. The difference between the kind of seed-bed required by wheat and that required by barley is due less to the differing demands of the plants themselves than to the fact that barley is sown in the spring, whereas wheat is sown in the autumn. The weathering during the winter will do much to reduce by the spring the condition of the land upon which wheat was sown to a state closely resembling a seed-bed suitable for barley. It would be just as undesirable to sow winter wheat in a tilth of 'onion bed' fineness as it would to sow barley in slop.

THEM AS BRINGS UP THE COWS SHOULD BE ONE LEGGED AND DUMB

The over-driving of dairy cows by noisy youngsters is all too common, and nothing is less conducive to production. A high-yielding dairy cow is a highly strung and sensitive creature which demands quiet and gentle treatment if she is to do her best. In fact gentleness is a fundamental characteristic of all good stockmen.

T A DOUBLE L DOESN'T SPELL BIG

A very old saying among horsemen to indicate that height at the withers is not the sole criterion of size; width, depth, and amount of bone being at least of equal importance. Presumably the expression 'a big little 'un' refers to a horse which, though not big in the sense of being tall, is big in every other way.

A GOOD BIG 'UN IS BETTER THAN A GOOD LITTLE 'UN

Though this refers particularly to horses, both light and heavy, I think it may be applied with advantage to other stock as well. Size with quality is unfortunately a rare combination. The majority of very large animals tend to be coarse. Unfortunately, there is an equal tendency for the 'quality' animal to be small, so much so that there is a real danger that some breeds may become no more than 'pretty toys'. While the out-sized, coarse beast is undesirable, the small 'all quality' animal is not less so, and in fact is probably even less profitable to its producer.

A GOOD ROOT YEAR IS A BAD SHEEP YEAR

Mr J. F. H. Thomas in his recently published book on sheep quotes this saw, which is a familiar one in those districts where it is customary to maintain breeding flocks of arable-land ewes. 'Such sayings as these', he says, 'usually have a sound foundation. It is at times very difficult to get some shepherds to realise that overfeeding with roots, when ewes are heavy in lamb, is a thoroughly bad practice.'

In seasons when the turnip crop is good there is a temptation to allow ewes more roots than they would normally receive, but invariably this is followed by trouble at lambing time; the lambs, though well grown, will be soft and a large number will die when very young.

History bears out the truth of this statement, in so far as all the really disastrous seasons recorded in this country have been disastrous by reason of excessive wet and never by reason of drought. A wet year is always a bad corn year, and though in such a season there may be an abundance of grass the stock fail to thrive.

Of course we in this country just do not know the meaning of the word drought as it is understood in some parts of the world—in Australia for example. There are, however, areas in England—areas mainly of arable land—where the weather can at times be very dry. But the driest of such seasons is to be preferred to a really wet one, even on the lighter soils.

There is another saw which has the same meaning and which emphasizes the fact that a dry season is not inimicable to corn:

'A dry summer never made a dear peck.'

THERE ARE THREE WAYS OF LOSING MONEY;
BACKING HORSES IS THE QUICKEST,
WINE AND WOMEN IS THE PLEASANTEST,
BUT FATTENING BULLOCKS IS THE SUREST

I do not claim that this is an old saw; in fact I am pretty sure it is not. Yet I make no apologies for including it. It refers, of course, to the winter fattening of cattle. It is doubtful if this old practice was ever directly profitable except in an occasional season when store cattle happened to be very cheap and beef was dear. In fact few Eastern Counties farmers, at any rate, ever expected to obtain any direct profit from their fat bullocks and were content if they paid for what they consumed, leaving behind them only 'their muck and their memory'.

Before the last war the diet of such cattle consisted of roots and straw, sometimes some seeds hay, plus a generous allowance of cake and corn. In this way two relays of cattle often passed through the yards in the course of the season. With the war, however, the rations of cake and corn had to be severely restricted with a consequent slowing up of the fattening process, and the old-fashioned system of 'time and turnips' had to be reverted to.

The big fattening bullock is ideal for the purpose of treading down straw on arable farms and making rich manure with which to maintain fertility. It is unfortunate, therefore, that winter fattening is not of itself profitable, for it means that it can be indulged in only when profits on crop production are high, or alternatively (in some cases) where, as a result of Excess Profits Tax, it may be carried on at the expense of the Chancellor of the Exchequer.

A GOOD PLOUGHING IS WORTH A COAT OF MUCK

The importance of good ploughing can hardly be over-emphasized, particularly when it is old turf that is being ploughed. This has been the universal experience during these last six years, and it is hardly an exaggeration to say that in such cases bad and indifferent ploughing has been one of the commonest causes of crop failure.

What constitutes good ploughing? The reply of ninety-nine per cent of people to this question would be that the furrows should be straight, as though this were the most important, and in fact the only requirement.

Culpin in his book on *Farm Machinery* gives the following as being among the more important requirements of good ploughing for British conditions:

1. All vegetation, manure, etc. should be completely covered.

2. The 'top' or ridge should be set up with no unploughed ground beneath it, at approximately the same height as the rest of the work.

3. All furrows should be straight and of a uniform depth and width. The furrow wall and bottom should be clean-cut.

4. The land should be left in the condition required. This may be either well set up with the slices unbroken and pressed together, or completely pulverized to full plough depth.

5. The furrow ends should be finished off evenly with no packed or unploughed soil, and the land should be finished off in a manner suited to the style and object of ploughing.

When dotterel do first appear
It shows that frost is very near;
But when the dotterel do go,
Then you may look for heavy snow

67

ONE WHITE LEG—BUY A HORSE,
TWO WHITE LEGS—TRY A HORSE,
THREE WHITE LEGS—LOOK WELL ABOUT HIM,
FOUR WHITE LEGS—DO WITHOUT HIM

Is this just prejudice, or is it indeed a fact that a horse with four white legs is to be avoided? Experience suggests that there may be something in it, and it is certain that such horses are unpopular. No explanation can, however, be offered; the only horse with four white legs that the writer ever owned was a very good-looking hunter mare and up to a lot of weight. She proved to be, however, what Mr Jorrocks would have described as a 'great henterpriseless brute wot would rayther 'ave a feed o' corn than the finest run wot ever was seen'. She was parted with without regret.

THE EARLY MAN NEVER BORROWS FROM THE LATE MAN

What I would describe as 'timeliness' is one of the most important factors in successful crop production. As Tusser says:

'Who soweth too lateward hath seldom good seed,
 Who soweth too soon, little better shall speed
 Apt time and the season, so diverse to hit,
 Let aier and layer help practice and wit.'

The word 'aier' refers to whatever depends on temperature and weather, while 'layer' refers to whatever depends upon tillage.

More often than not late sowing leads to a poor crop and to a late harvest. A vicious circle is thus established and continues from year to year. Some farmers are always behind, have been behind for years, and are likely to remain behind.

IF THE GRASS GROWS GREEN IN JANIVEER, IT GROWS THE WORSE FOR ALL THE YEAR

There is no evidence as to the truth of this adage, any more than there is to that of the saw which declares that a green Christmas makes a full churchyard. It does, however, seem as though a grass field will grow a certain amount of grass in a year and no more, but that the distribution of this growth from month to month varies from year to year. Thus, for example, if the spring is a dry one and the grass is short in May and June in consequence, then the amount of autumn growth will be correspondingly increased.

THE MASTER'S FOOT IS THE BEST MANURE

This saw—which has come to be almost a proverb—needs no explanation. It does, however, raise the question as to how much land one man can efficiently manage, for clearly when one man farms many thousands of acres of arable land it can get but a small share of the master's foot, though it may get a fair share of his eye (generally from a car) which is not at all the same thing.

Admittedly the majority of these very large holdings are well and efficiently farmed, but that is probably not so much because of their size as because they are farmed by exceptionally able men, most of whom started in a small way and as a result of their success and ability gradually added farm to farm. These men will probably be the first to admit that there is an optimum size for any farming enterprise which if exceeded leads to decreased efficiency, and though the decrease may be small yet it is progressive. When a holding exceeds a certain area it necessarily receives less and less of its master's foot, and, though he may employ competent managers, yet the manager's foot is not the master's.

There is an alternative rendering of this saw: 'The presence of the master is the profit of the field.'

Tusser has the same idea in his verse:

> 'The eye of the master enricheth the hutch,
> The eye of the mistress availeth as much;
> Which eye, if it govern, with reason and skill,
> Hath servant and service, at pleasure and will.'

WHEN THE CUCKOO SINGS ON AN EMPTY BOUGH, KEEP YOUR HAY AND SELL YOUR COW

The empty bough presumably means a bough without leaves, which would indicate a late and backward season. In such a season grass will be in short supply; hence the advice to conserve your hay and reduce your stock. It is possible that there may be some other interpretation, but if so it is obscure.

YOU CAN BURN DOCKS BUT THE ASHES WILL GROW

As this saw indicates, the dock is one of the most troublesome weeds to eradicate; it is one of those vexatious plants that spread not only vegetatively but also by means of seed as well. Almost any little piece of its thick, fleshy root will grow if left in the land, but, even when all the roots have been collected and burnt, there is still the seed in the soil to be reckoned with. This seed seems capable of remaining dormant for long periods, finally germinating when conditions are favourable.

A FARM THAT HAS GUINEA-FOWLS HAS NO RATS

I have not the least idea what was the origin of this belief; nor can I find the slightest evidence of its truth. I suppose it might be argued that guinea-fowl are such good scavengers that even a rat cannot pick up a living behind them, or alternatively that rats just cannot endure the guinea-fowl's irritating cry! But since the belief has no foundation in fact, no explanation is required.

MUCK IS LUCK

It is frequently said that good luck is only another term for good management, and muck is luck for much the same reason. A farm where there is always plenty of farmyard manure is a farm which carries a lot of stock, where the straw, hay, roots and much of the corn is consumed at home and finds its way back to the land again in the form of muck. Land which is thus kept in good heart can be relied upon to grow good crops under conditions which would spell failure on land less well done. It is indeed 'lucky' land.

'Muck is luck' is probably a modern corruption of Tusser's version:

> 'The better the muck
> The better good luck.'

Here the stress is upon the *quality* of the manure, though in comparison with modern standards the quality of the muck available in Tusser's day can never have been very high, for no cake was obtainable and no corn for cattle feeding could be spared. In the absence of roots, cake and corn, no winter fattening was possible, hence really rich manure as we understand it to-day simply did not exist. Presumably the quality of the manure in those days was judged by its degree of rottenness for Tusser goes on to say:

> 'Whose campas is rotten, and carried in time,
> And spread as it should be, thrifts' ladder may climb,
> Whose campas is paltry, and carried too late,
> Such husbandry useth as many do hate.'

SHEEP MAY BE STARVED IN TWO WAYS—TOO MANY TO THE ACRE OR TOO FEW

That sheep may be starved by overstocking is obvious, but it is not so obvious how they may be starved by understocking. Yet this is certainly true. Sheep cannot compete with long, rank, coarse growth, they do best on short fine grass. If a field is fed exclusively by a few sheep which are quite insufficient in number to keep it grazed down, the grass will inevitably grow away from them, and if this treatment is persisted in long enough then the amount of food that the field will grow which is suited to sheep becomes progressively less until ultimately the point will be reached when the field provides an insufficient amount of food, even for the few sheep it contains.

GOOD HARVESTS MAKE MEN PRODIGAL, BAD ONES PROVIDENT

One of the results of the large profits made by farmers during the 1914–18 war was that it encouraged extravagance and raised the standard of living to a point at which it could not be sustained. This has been vividly described in Mr A. G. Street's popular book *Farmer's Glory*.

Farmers are perhaps unique in that after a good harvest, when money is plentiful, they tend to spend a large part of it on their farms, by carrying out various improvements, purchasing new implements and so on. This is commendable and very much to the good up to a point, though sometimes the economies so effected do not really justify the expenditure. A prudent man will consider the economics of spending say five hundred pounds just as carefully at a time when he is prosperous and has money in the bank as he will when money is scarce.

I once had an old farmer friend who having started farming in the eighties retired in 1915, just before the prosperous war years. Practically the whole of his farming had been done during a period of agricultural depression. Yet he retired with a comfortable fortune, all of which he made out of farming. It is true that he was a good farmer and farmed a useful farm of some 800 acres, yet very few of his contemporaries, equally good farmers and farming on an equally large scale, were ever in a financial position to retire. I asked him if he could explain to me how this was, and he unhesitatingly replied that it was because, after a good year when he had made money, he withdrew what he had made from the bank and invested it—usually I believe in mortgages, whereas most of his fellows, when they had had a good year and saw a substantial balance at the bank, spent it freely on expensive improvements, which never really paid them.

THERE IS GOOD LAND WHERE THERE IS
A FOUL WAY

Up to some seventy years or so ago the test of good land in this country was whether it would grow wheat. Wheat was then *the* crop; it had always been wanted, it seemed certain that it always would be wanted, and as it was a profitable crop to grow it was argued that land which would grow it well must be valuable land. Now, while it is true that wheat will grow on a wide range of soils, yet it thrives best on the heavier classes of land. The state of the roads one hundred years ago in clay-land areas in the days before roads were metalled is proverbial. From all accounts 'foul' is a very restrained description of what they were like.

To-day the test of good land is no longer its capacity to grow wheat. The bursar of every Cambridge college could give examples of farms left to the college by pious benefactors a hundred and fifty or so years ago which at the time were very valuable properties, but whose value has dropped to a mere fraction of what it then was. These farms are almost without exception composed of clay-land—land which being situated in a relatively dry area will grow wheat admirably, but unfortunately is suited to very little else.

Yet it may still be true even to-day that there is good land where there is a foul way, for what we consider our best land to-day is devoted to the growing of crops such as potatoes which involve a great deal of carting, and much carting, particularly in winter, often implies a foul way.

EARLY SOW, EARLY MOW

This applies particularly to spring-sown corn, though it does not mean that barley sown on 1 March will be ready to cut a month before barley sown on 1 April. If both sowings are the same variety then that sown at the earlier date will certainly be ripe some time sooner, but not a month sooner, for the later sowing, sown at a time when the land is warmer, will grow more rapidly and will tend to catch up that which was sown early.

In these days the date of ripening of a crop depends as much or even more upon the variety which is sown than on the date of sowing, for there are now available a wide range of quick-growing and rapidly maturing varieties by means of which time lost at sowing can, within limits, be made up.

The date of sowing winter corn has very little influence upon the date of harvesting, the difference of a month in the date of sowing may mean no more than two or three days' difference in the date of harvesting. In the case of wheat the choice of variety is all important in this connection. Where combine harvesters are used it is very desirable that the various fields of wheat should not all ripen together. The desire of farmers who rely upon combines to avoid this and to ensure that the ripening of their various wheat fields is spread over as long a period as possible, is the chief consideration which governs their choice of what varieties they shall sow.

IF CORN IS CHEAP STOCK IS NEVER DEAR

This is not to say that when corn is unprofitable stock is also unprofitable, for even though the price of stock may not be high yet if feeding-stuffs are very cheap the cost of meat production may be so low that it may still leave a fair margin of profit. This of course is most marked with those classes of stock such as pigs whose diet includes a high proportion of purchased feeding-stuffs. With pigs, for example, expenditure on food represents something like eighty per cent of the total cost of production. There was a time in the early nineteen-thirties when it was possible to purchase almost all feeding-stuffs at a lower cost than they could be grown on the farm. The tendency was, therefore, for farmers to grow less and less and buy more and more, and in fact to become processors rather than producers, converting large quantities of raw material (purchased feeding-stuffs) into the finished product (meat). That this was a thoroughly unhealthy and undesirable development must be admitted, but it was one for which farmers were not responsible.

FAMINE ALWAYS BEGINS IN THE HORSE'S MANGER

No doubt in the old days this would be so, for a horse, having a small stomach, when it is in full work, requires a comparatively concentrated diet containing a high proportion of corn which could alternatively be fed directly into human stomachs. If the choice lay between starving horses and starving men there is no doubt which would be preferred, though how the work of ploughing and sowing would be carried out the following spring with a lot of starved and weak horses it is difficult to understand.

When ant-hills are unusually high in July it betokens a hard and long winter

Up to the time of the formation of the Pig Marketing Board in 1933 the fluctuations in the price of pork were proverbial, and the price varied in inverse ratio with the pig population. When the pig population was high the price of pig-meat fell, and when the fall had reached the point at which it was no longer profitable to produce them farmers hurriedly gave up their pigs and reduced their breeding stock. Ultimately the time arrived when pigs became scarce and dear once more with the result that the high profits made by those who still had pigs to sell were sufficient to attract farmers to begin breeding pigs again, and the whole cycle recommenced.

That this rapid fluctuation in the population is confined to pigs, and is not found in cattle or sheep is explained by the prolificacy of the pig as compared with other classes of stock. A sow may well rear sixteen pigs a year in two litters; of these half will be females which themselves may be producing young at some thirteen months old. A cow, on the other hand, will only produce one calf a year at most, which means one heifer in two years, and it will be three years before the heifer herself will produce a calf.

The object of the Pig Marketing Board was to stabilize the price of pig-meat at a reasonable and profitable level so that the pig population could be stabilized. In this it succeeded up to 1939 when the outbreak of war and the difficulty of importing feeding-stuffs and the need to conserve home-grown corn for human consumption made it impossible to maintain the pig population.

COCKSFOOT IS A GOOD SERVANT BUT A BAD MASTER

Cocksfoot is one of our most valuable pasture grasses. It provides an abundance of excellent food, and has the advantage of being relatively deep-rooted so that it will stand drought better than most grasses. Moreover, it provides quite a lot of valuable winter food, particularly for sheep. Properly managed it thus has everything to commend it. On the other hand, if it is badly managed, undergrazed and allowed to get out of hand, it may ruin what would otherwise be a good pasture. When undergrazed it becomes coarse and tends to tuftiness, so much so that it has a bad name among some farmers but never among those who keep a breeding flock of grassland ewes.

LIME, MANURE AND VIGOROUS CLOVER
MAKES THE FARM'S LAND RICH ALL OVER

Up to a few years ago a leguminous crop was the pivotal crop in every rotation, and was taken regularly every fourth or fifth year. Leguminous crops were the chief means by which the nitrogen supplies of the soil were replenished. Anything, therefore, which encouraged their growth was beneficial to the crops of the whole rotation. Clover, and indeed all leguminous crops, will flourish only when the lime status of the soil is satisfactory. Consequently, on many soils where lime is apt to be deficient, the first step that must be taken if a leguminous crop is to be grown successfully is to lime it. But lime alone is not sufficient to ensure a crop of vigorous clover.

Oddly enough, in spite of the fact that they alone among plants have the power of obtaining their supplies of nitrogen from the atmosphere, legumes respond better than most plants to generous dressings of farmyard manure. If land is well supplied with lime and has been regularly manured, then leguminous crops will flourish and will in their turn still further raise its fertility.

SATURDAY NEW, SUNDAY FULL, NEVER NO GOOD, AND NEVER 'ULL

Why a moon which is new on a Saturday and full on a Sunday should be supposed to be so unlucky I have no idea, nor is there any indication if it betokens misfortune generally or merely a period of bad weather.

ILL WEEDS GROW APACE

This is literally true as well as being true metaphorically. A weed which has become much more troublesome of late years —particularly in sugar-beet growing areas—is goosefoot or 'fat hen' as it is sometimes called. This is a perfect example of an ill weed growing apace, for it seems to grow inches in a single night! Root fields which have been well hoed right up to the time of corn harvest and which are then perfectly clean, may be covered with 'fat hen' by the time harvest is over, and labour for weeding is again available.

MARCH DUST TO BE SOLD
WORTH RANSOM OF GOLD

There is an alternative version which goes:

> 'A bushel of March dust is a thing
> Worth the ransom of a king.'

A dry March is a tremendous boon, particularly to farmers of heavy land. It is important that spring corn should be sown in a perfect seed-bed; it is no less important that it should be sown in good time. If March is wet these two ideals are unattainable. Another advantage of a dry March is that it allows of cleaning operations on land that is to be planted with roots in April. It is highly beneficial from every point of view. As another saying has it: 'A dry March never begs its bread.'

KILL IT TO SAVE ITS LIFE

If a carcass is to be of any use for human food the animal must have been slaughtered and bled in the proper way. It sometimes happens that as a result of an accident an animal is mortally hurt. If before it dies as a result of its injuries it can be slaughtered and bled in the ordinary way the carcass may (particularly if the animal is fat) have considerable value, as it will be fit for human consumption, whereas if the animal is allowed to die the carcass will be virtually valueless. Hence the expression.

Animals which are injured but are not mortally wounded and which would in course of time recover are frequently slaughtered if they happen to be in good condition at the time of the accident. Any animal that suffers pain will rapidly lose flesh, and it is better business to slaughter it at once, even if a lower price per stone has to be accepted for the carcass, than to allow it to recover and start fattening it all over again.

It should be noted that there is the qualification that the animal must be fat, or at least in forward condition if it is to be slaughtered. Flesh from animals which are slaughtered in 'store' condition has little value as human food. Owing to the absence of marbling fat (the fatty tissue which runs in 'veins' between the muscle fibres and which gives good meat the appearance of marble) the meat from such animals will be tough, dry and flavourless—fit only for hounds. Animals are fattened before slaughter not for the sake of lumps of tallow but in order to obtain this marbling fat without which the meat is unpalatable.

LONG FORETOLD, LONG LAST, SHORT NOTICE, SOON PAST

Of all the adages which refer to the weather this is the one which is the most reliable. When the barometer either rises or falls slowly and steadily a long spell either of fine settled weather or of bad weather usually follows. On the other hand, if the glass rises or falls very rapidly the resulting period of fine or wet weather is likely to be only of short duration.

ONE FOR SORROW, TWO FOR MIRTH,
THREE FOR A WEDDING, FOUR FOR A BIRTH,
FIVE FOR SILVER, SIX FOR GOLD,
SEVEN IS A TALE THAT HAS NEVER BEEN TOLD

Magpies seem to have increased in numbers during these last few years—no doubt due to the fact that the number of game-keepers has been reduced. But even in the days when magpies were comparatively scarce (and there were large areas where up to thirty years ago they were almost non-existent), it was unusual to see one alone. Evidently there is a great deal less sorrow than mirth in the world! I have always understood, however, that the ill omen of a single magpie could be largely counteracted if one were particularly polite to the bird, taking off one's hat and bidding it good-day.

Precisely what is the meaning of the last line I do not know, but a few years ago I encountered, one winter's day, a flock of forty-odd magpies on the edge of the Cambridgeshire fens, and still live to tell the tale!

WHEN IN DOUBT SOW SQUAREHEADS MASTER

Squareheads Master is the name of a variety of wheat that has been in cultivation for pretty well a century. New varieties come and new varieties go but Squareheads Master remains a prime favourite, and for the good reason that it will give a useful crop over a wider range of soils and conditions that any other wheat. Some wheats are at home only on heavy land, others will thrive on light. Some wheats prefer a moist climate, others a dry. Some wheats are delicate and will only yield well under optimum conditions and at high levels of fertility, while others will give a fair crop under conditions that are very far removed from the optimum.

No doubt there is (theoretically at least) a variety of wheat best suited to each individual field. It is, however, impracticable, except on very large farms, for a farmer to grow more than two or three different varieties on his farm, hence the value of Squareheads Master which suits such a wide range of soil and conditions. There is one set of conditions, however, for which Squareheads Master is unsuitable. It is inclined to have long weak straw, and as a result, on good land in a high state of fertility it often lodges badly. Its lack of standing power is its worst fault. There are now, however, plenty of new varieties which have been bred expressly for these particular conditions, high-yielding varieties with short, stiff straw which, if sown on good land in a high state of fertility, will far out-yield Squareheads Master. In fact, a disproportionate number of the new varieties seem to have been bred with these conditions in view. What is required now are varieties which will give improved yields when grown on average land in average conditions.

A fog in summer is followed by heat, in autumn by rain, in winter by frost

Peter Beckford would certainly have agreed for he wrote: 'The colour I think of little moment; and am of opinion with our friend Foote, respecting his negro friend, that a good dog, like a good candidate, cannot be a bad colour.'

But while it is no doubt true that a good horse is a good horse whatever its colour, yet it does not follow that the proportion of good horses among those of certain unpopular colours may not be very low. This at least is generally supposed to be the case, and there are strong prejudices against certain colours in all classes of stock. Generally speaking pale colours are disliked, 'washy' chestnuts for example among horses, and 'washy' roans and 'lemony' reds among cattle as opposed to rich roans and blood reds—this in spite of there being some evidence that the proportion of good milkers among lemony-red cows is greater than that among blood reds. Undoubtedly there are fashions in colours, and a colour which is popular to-day may be unpopular to-morrow. For example, black was a very popular colour among Shire horses years ago, but is rarely seen to-day. Again 'broken' colours, and white markings are not fashionable to-day with breeders of Jersey cattle for no apparent reason.

Sometimes an outstanding individual of a certain colour will popularize it, and of course any great and outstanding sire may influence the colour of a whole breed. A good example of this was the thoroughbred stallion, The Tetrarch, which was responsible for a large number of grey descendants, but before whose advent grey was a colour that was rarely seen on a racecourse.

Of course, certain colours are characteristic of certain breeds and it is natural that any departures from such colour should be viewed with suspicion, though they do admittedly occur even among the best-bred stock. For example, a red Aberdeen Angus calf is sometimes born, a brown and white Friesian, and a bay or brown Percheron. These are examples of 'off' colours and are not to be confused with 'bad' colours. Red and white is not a popular colour among Shorthorn breeders, particularly when the white is splashed in large patches, nor is a pure white, though for this there is a reason, there being a complaint known as 'white heifer disease' which is confined to females of this colour.

HIGH FARMING IS NO REMEDY FOR LOW PRICES

This dictum of Lawes has been repeated so often that it has almost become a proverb. Pliny, writing some nineteen hundred years earlier, made a somewhat similar statement: 'Nihil minus expedire quam agrum optime colere...!' (Nothing is less profitable than to cultivate land to perfection). But Lawes' dictum has all too often been torn from its context and has been quoted in defence of a level of farming well below that warranted by the prevailing level of prices. In his original paper in which he discusses the Rothamsted experiments Lawes wrote: 'The general and uniform result of the whole is that whether we go from *high to higher* farming... with large amounts of farmyard manure...or with artificial manure in gradually increasing amounts, less increase of production is obtained for a given amount of manure.'

The point which I would stress is that the range of intensity of the farming about which Lawes was speaking was high to higher, *not* low to high. While it is true that the climax, when the extra crop obtained ceases to pay for manures or labour expended on it, is sooner reached with low than with high prices, yet it can be safely said that this point was but rarely reached on most British farms between the two wars.

The degree of intensity with which any particular area of land can be farmed profitably depends not only upon the prevailing price level but also upon the land's inherent fertility. The highest farming will be found on the best land during periods of agricultural prosperity. At such a time the law of diminishing returns does not operate except at an abnormally high level of production and the farmer can afford to spend large sums on labour and fertilizers in order to obtain the last bushel which his land is capable of yielding. The other extreme is the marginal land, land of inherently low fertility, which when prices are very low will not pay to farm at all and which, as a result, either tumbles down to rough grazing or is just abandoned.

It is certainly true that with such land, during a time of agricultural depression, any attempt to improve the position by an intensification of production is doomed to failure. On the other hand, between the two wars, there was a great deal of land in this country which would have been far more profitable if it had been better farmed. The low level of the farming on much of our land was not justified by the price of produce.

NE'ER CAST A CLOUT
TILL MAY IS OUT

In a fickle climate no doubt the advice is sound, but every few years, with the utmost regularity, there is a heated newspaper controversy as to whether May refers to the month of May or the blossom. I have a completely open mind on the subject myself, and in any case the point will shortly be of academic interest only for with the present (1947) meagre ration of clothing coupons we shall soon have no clouts to cast!

WHEN EAGER BITES THE THIRSTY FLEA
CLOUDS AND RAIN YOU SURE SHALL SEE

Lack of experience leaves me unable to say what truth there is in this rhyme; I must, therefore, leave it to those of my readers who are in a position to judge for themselves.

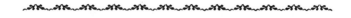

COLD MAY AND WINDY,
BARN FILLETH UP FINELY

No weather suits all cases alike; a dry, cold May may suit corn—certainly it will suit it better than a wet one, but it will not suit grass and in any case needs to be followed by a dripping June if it is to benefit corn. In this connection 'wet May—long hay' and 'Dry May and dripping June put all things in tune' are two adages which are contradictory.

I once had an old horsekeeper who about the second week in June always used to say to me: 'Well, Master, I reckon we've got the weather cornered now. If it's fine we can get on with the hay, and if it's wet it'll do the roots a world of good.' Unfortunately, he wasn't right: we found we hadn't always got the weather cornered after all, for sometimes we had about then a week or two of dull, drizzly weather when there was insufficient rain to do the roots much good, but enough to prevent us from getting on with hay-making!

MANY A GOOD COW HAS A BAD CALF

It seems a little unfair to put the entire blame upon the cow; presumably the bull is equally responsible! But even when a good bull is mated to a good cow the result is not always a good calf, though undoubtedly the chances are very much improved. Animal breeding is still more of an art than a science, and it is likely to remain an art for many years to come, for which some of us are devoutly thankful. Moreover, there is always an element of chance about it, which perhaps is part of its attraction!

LOVE THY NEIGHBOUR, BUT PULL NOT DOWN THY HEDGE

This saying requires no explanation and is so apt that it is surprising that it is not more widely known or more often quoted.

There is no relation between the rent usually charged for really good land and that charged for land of poor or average quality. This is no doubt to what the saying refers. The poorer classes of land are relatively much dearer than land of the better sorts. The difference in rent between the two rarely exceeds 30s. an acre. There was never any doubt as to which was the cheaper years ago—the type of land let at 15s. an acre or that for which 40s. was obtained. With the costs of production steadily rising, and rent being the only item included in those costs in which there has been little change, it follows that the discrepancy is greater to-day than ever before. There was a time—not so long ago—when rent was the largest single item in the list of the farmer's total annual expenditure. Its place has now been taken by the wages bill which on most farms far exceeds the rent.

Good land is more profitable to farm than poor land, not only because the yields obtained from it are greater without any proportionate increase in costs of working, but also because they are more certain. One of the greatest disadvantages of poor land is its susceptibility to seasonal effects. On such land yields fluctuate wildly from year to year. No land, however good or however well farmed, is immune to the effect of season, but on the best lands the fluctuations are comparatively small. It would hardly be an exaggeration to say that immunity to season is the most valuable characteristic of good land. If good land is admittedly so much cheaper than poor land, and so much more profitable, how is it that

rents do not adjust themselves? To this question there seems
to be no answer. The fact remains that many farmers who
will willingly pay a rent of 20*s*. an acre for a farm of just
useful land, will hesitate before they will offer 50*s*. for land
very much better.

There is another sense in which rent is the cheapest thing
that a farmer buys. Compare the amount of stock food a
farmer obtains from a 20-acre grass field for which he pays
£50 a year rent with the amount of food which he can purchase for the same sum spent in any other way.

A PLANT A STRIDE,
LET 'UN BIDE

Some of the most difficult decisions that a farmer is ever
called upon to make concern thin plants. Shall a plant which
is thin be left in the hope that it will improve and thicken, or
should it be ploughed up and a fresh start made? If he decides
to plough it up the farmer will never know if his decision was
right or not; if on the other hand he leaves it, hoping for the
best, he may live to regret it, or alternatively to congratulate
himself on the wisdom of his choice. Experience of his own
land will be his best guide. With good land in good heart it
is remarkable how a thin plant in the early spring will gather
and spread as the season advances.

One would guess from the words that this couplet emanates
from the west country, and would apply to its rich red
loams. Under such conditions a thin plant might very well

be left with advantage. The best crop of wheat that I ever grew—25 acres which yielded 73 bushels per acre—was so thin a plant that I seriously debated ploughing it up early in March but gave it the benefit of the doubt. Had I ploughed it up no doubt I should still believe that I had done right!

On poor land, particularly if it is in a low state of cultivation, a thin plant will often go from bad to worse. The unfortunate thing is that the resulting loss is not confined to the loss of just that one crop, for a thin crop is always a foul one, and at the end of the season the farmer is left to mourn not only the loss of a crop but also a foul field. This perhaps is one of the worst features of a thin plant and makes the decision whether to leave it or plough it up so important. One of the strongest arguments in favour of high farming is the fact that heavy crops automatically mean clean land. Nature abhors a vacuum, and vacant spaces in any piece of land which are not filled with crop will soon be filled with something else.

Tusser realized the truth of this when he wrote:

> 'See corn sown in,
> Too thick, nor too thin.
> For want of seed,
> Land yieldeth weed.'

In these days economy of seed is not by any means the chief reason for thin plants, but rather indifferent seed-beds, the depredations of vermin, and (commonest of all) late sowing.

Ne'er trust a July sky

WHEN A FARMER STARTS GROWING RYE IT IS TIME FOR HIS CREDITORS TO COLLECT THEIR DEBTS

This is a recognition of the fact that rye will yield some sort of a crop on land which is in a very low state of fertility. It is as it were the last hope of the destitute. If the lighter classes of land are to grow wheat successfully they need to be well farmed; indeed such lands require very special preparation if a good crop of wheat is to be grown. In the case of a farmer who is going bankrupt his financial condition is inevitably reflected in the state of his farm, and his land, which when it was well farmed would grow wheat, will reach a point when it will grow nothing better than rye—and only a poor crop of that. This is the time for his creditors to step in, for it is the beginning of the end.

The length of time that a farmer can hang on while he is in process of going bankrupt is one of the tragic features of the farming industry. He may be going slowly but surely bankrupt for ten years or more and the tragedy is that his land will suffer. At the end his farm will be foul and starved, with overgrown hedges, neglected ditches and dilapidated buildings. No one wants to follow him on the farm for it will take a long time and much money to make good all the damage that has been done.

A SHELTER IS AS GOOD AS A FEED

Large numbers of cattle in this country are regularly out-wintered. They depend for their food partly upon rough grass and when this is exhausted, and during periods of stormy weather, upon hay and straw which is carried to them in the fields. Such cattle grow long shaggy coats of hair which protect them from wet as well as from cold. Sometimes open sheds are provided for them, but they are not as a rule very much used by the cattle which seem to prefer to remain outside except when the wind is particularly bitter. These sheds, however, are often filled with racks so that hay may be fed under cover, and for this purpose they are useful as much waste is thus prevented.

The shelter mentioned in the saying probably refers to natural shelter, shelter provided by hedges and plantations. Such shelter is regularly used by outwintering stock and is much appreciated by them. It enables them to get out of the wind and driving rain, and there is no doubt that cattle so provided will thrive better than cattle which are exposed to the full fury of the weather, even though these latter may be provided with extra food.

NO MAN CAN TAKE OUT OF THE LAND MORE THAN HE PUTS IN

Ultimately, of course, this is true, though there are men who will, if they get the opportunity, hire a farm in good heart— one that has been well farmed for many years—and farm it out, taking everything they can get from the land and putting nothing back. This is not farming but land robbery, and there is a world of difference between the two. Unfortunately, such a farm may be worth twice as much rent to rob for a few years as it is to farm. This explains how it is that such men are ever able to hire such farms. It is, however, a most short-sighted policy on the part of the landlord to accept a land robber as a tenant whatever rent he offers.

The classic case of land robbery was the growing of wheat on the virgin soils of America. The land was cropped with wheat year after year and nothing was returned to the soil, not even the straw. The *apparent* cost of wheat grown in this way was only a fraction of the cost of wheat grown under conditions where the fertility of the land was maintained simultaneously, and it was this wheat, sold here at a very low price, which ruined many of our farmers. The *real* cost of the wheat, however, was very different from the *apparent* cost, for to the apparent cost has to be added the capital value of millions of acres of land which were ruined in the process. The 'dust bowl' in America is a standing memorial to the truth of this saying that no man can take out of the land more than he puts in.

GRANT SOIL HER LUST,
SOW RYE IN DUST

Rye grown for grain as distinct from rye grown for forage is confined to the poorer types of light land. It is a crop that may be grown successfully on land which is too light for any other autumn-sown cereal and has the additional advantage that it will tolerate a considerable degree of acidity. On such land early sowing is essential if a good crop is to be obtained, and much rye is sown quite early in September. By reason of its nature and the time of year the soil is likely to be dry and dusty when the crop is sown.

Tusser says:

> 'Sow timely thy white wheat, sow rye in the dust,
> Let seed have his longing, let soil have her lust;
> Let rye be partaker of Michelmas spring,
> To bear out the hardness that winter doth bring.'

EVERY MOVE A SHEEP MAKES SHOULD BE A MOVE FOR THE BETTER

In this country the majority of sheep are not fattened on the farms where they are bred, but are sold as 'store' lambs by their breeders and are purchased by farmers who are 'feeders', or the purchasers may keep them for some time as stores and then pass them on again to farms where they will ultimately be fattened.

The saying makes the point that if these sheep are to thrive (and therefore prove profitable) they must always move on to better land. No experienced farmer who knows his business will buy sheep, however attractive, which come from land better than his own. If he does the sheep, instead of improving, will go back in condition unless they are fed on an expensive ration of cake and corn. What applies to sheep for fattening applies equally to ewes intended for breeding. The Border Leicester × Cheviot, the North Country half-bred as it is commonly called, is a case in point. Large numbers of these ewes move south every year and are very popular, not only because of their prolificacy and mothering qualities, but also because of the way that they themselves improve as a result of the better conditions to which they come. Even mature mountain ewes of the regular draught will change almost beyond recognition in the course of a few weeks when they are moved from their native hills on to good lowland pastures.

What is true of sheep is true too, though in a lesser degree, of cattle. Of all classes of stock sheep are the most influenced by their environment, but store cattle off poor hill-land do noticeably better than cattle from superior land.

SOW BEANS IN THE MUD
AND THEY'LL GROW LIKE A WOOD

They *may* grow like a wood, but on the other hand my experience is they may not, and even if they do it doesn't follow that they will pod well and that a good yield of beans will ultimately result. It is quite unsafe to estimate the yield of a crop of beans until shortly before it is fit to cut, and even then it is difficult to judge with accuracy. A great deal of straw is rarely associated with a heavy yield of beans.

Beans has been the most disappointing crop that we have grown during the war. Now that farmers have to be largely self-supporting in animal feeding-stuffs it is a crop of considerable importance for beans and peas are the only crops that a farmer can grow that will provide him with a high protein concentrate. It is most unfortunate therefore that they have done so badly. Our grandfathers seem to have been much more successful with beans than we are to-day. Various reasons have been advanced to account for this, but none of them are very convincing. It is true that our fore-bears always dunged for beans and carefully hand hoed them in the spring; but even where this is done now the crop is still often very poor. Of course the disease known as chocolate pot ruins many of our crops to-day, a disease which seems to have been unknown years ago, but chocolate spot does not by any means account for the poor yields obtained in every case. It may be that we have lost the varieties which our grandfathers cultivated so successfully. The bean is a plant which cross fertilizes, and it is therefore exceedingly difficult to keep any variety pure for long. Continued re-selection seems necessary.

NO GOOD FARMER WHEN HE LEAVES A FARM IS EVER SUFFICIENTLY REWARDED, AND NO BAD FARMER IS EVER SUFFICIENTLY PENALIZED

This has always been recognized ever since 'tenant right' was first instituted. That it should be so is unfair and unjust, and has the unfortunate result, in some cases at least, of farmers deliberately letting down the standard of cultivation of their holdings for the last few years of their tenancy. 'Farming for a get out' is an expression which is still heard far too often. Those good farmers (and they are the majority) who cannot bring themselves to do this are out of pocket as a result.

The remedy lies with tenant right valuers. Until the sum in which an outgoing tenant is mulct for dilapidations bears a closer relationship to the cost of making the dilapidations good, and until the value of what the good farmer leaves behind receives its due reward, so long will this maxim remain true.

MAY KITTENS NEVER MAKE GOOD CATS

It is impossible to say what is the origin of this belief. I should be surprised if it were true—if it is then the cat is unique among animals, for all young animals do best if they are born in the spring. This is not a question of temperature but of food supply, and in this connection the cat is no exception to the rule. From May onwards there are plenty of young birds, rabbits, rats and mice about which fall an easy prey to the mother cat and ensure a generous diet both for her and her offspring, which will then be reared on an optimum plane of nutrition. It may be, however, that I am confusing *good* cats with *fine* cats. A generous diet when young will ensure a fine cat, but it will not, I suppose, ensure a good cat in the sense that a good cat is one that is a good mouser and ratter. One would imagine, however, that a fine, strong, well-nourished kitten would be more likely to grow into a good ratter than a starveling.

THE YOUNGER THE STOCK THE NEARER
THE PLOUGH

This saying comes from the North of England where ley farming has been practised for many years. It emphasizes the fact that the younger classes of stock will thrive better on leys than on old permanent pastures. There are two or three reasons why this is so. In the first place, the best and richest old fattening pastures are too 'strong' for young cattle. Not only do young cattle on such pastures fail to thrive, but they scour so badly that if they are not removed quickly it may actually kill them. Young cattle do better on new pastures than on old not merely because the nutritive value of the grass is higher, is less fibrous and therefore more suitable for them, but also because young pastures are much 'cleaner' than old and far less likely to infect the young cattle with internal parasites from which they suffer far more than is generally suspected.

THERE IS MORE HAY SPOILED IN GOOD
WEATHER THAN IN BAD

This is no doubt an exaggeration but there is some truth in it. It is certainly quite easy to spoil hay in good weather by over-eagerness to save it before the weather changes. During hot, sunny weather its condition can be very deceptive, and at such a time it can easily be stacked before it is sufficiently dry, with the result that it heats badly and the stack has to be 'turned' (a thing which many farmers are ashamed to do and for which they will be teased unmercifully by all their friends and neighbours), or it may catch fire. The number of stack fires that occur after a spell of hot dry weather during the time of hay-making is proof of the truth of this.

But this is not the only way in which hay may be spoiled during good weather. At such a time it is sometimes over-made, and indeed in these days, when hay-making has been so largely mechanized and cocking (at least in the south-east) is a thing of the past, this is what frequently happens. Hay should never be exposed for long to the full power of the sun. If it is it will soon lose its colour, the leaf will become brittle and fall off as soon as ever the hay is touched, and the resulting material will be brown, stalky, flavourless and of low-feeding value.

Too often in these days hay-making consists simply of cutting the hay, turning it once or twice, and then sweeping it up straight into the stack. This method may be cheap, but it is not the way to make good hay. During fine weather, however, it is the method commonly adopted to-day on many large farms, and bad is made worse when the mower is allowed to get too far ahead, with the result that the mown hay is exposed to the sun and wind for several days longer than is necessary.

A ring round the sun in bad weather indicates
a speedy improvement

The partridge is the perfect game bird, it does no harm to the farmer (in fact it does good even when present in large numbers) and it provides sport to suit everyone. When walked up it is reasonably easy to shoot, and when driven very difficult—particularly with the wind behind it! Yet it is the commonest of all our game birds. It is as popular on the table as in the field, even if it has not quite so much meat on its thighs as a woodcock. There is nothing in the world better to eat than a plump young roasted partridge, the only complaint about it I have ever heard being that while half a partridge is not quite enough a whole one is too much—I cannot say that I have ever found it so!

The woodcock, on the other hand, is comparatively rare. In the open it provides a fairly easy shot, though in cover it has an amazing knack of getting a tree between itself and its pursuer. In spite of its scarcity it has probably been the cause of more accidents than all the other game birds put together—in fact at the cry of 'woodcock' one of my friends always throws himself flat on the ground and counts ten before he gets up! Of course it is an excellent bird to eat, though partridge is more to the taste of most people.

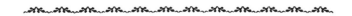

If the wind follows the sun fine weather
may be expected

The up-to-date version might well be: 'If you haven't got a tractor you must use horses!' During these last six years the tractor has become so relied upon to do the heavy work on the farm that there is a real danger of farmers thinking that there is no other means of doing it. In some counties there has been a tendency for farmers who do not own a tractor to sit back and wait for the War Agricultural Committee's tractor to plough their land for them. While it is true that ploughing by tractor is cheaper than ploughing by horses, yet the additional cost of horse ploughing may be well repaid if it means getting the land ploughed in good time rather than waiting one's turn.

A morning sun never lasts the day

★

*If March comes in like a lion
It goes out like a lamb*

★

*If the Dog days be clear
'Twill be fine all the year*

★

An early winter, a surly winter

★

*When the peacock loudly calls
Soon we'll have both rain and squalls*

★

*When cattle lie much rain is to be expected
When cattle walk much fine weather*

★

*Rain before seven
Fine before eleven*

Mackerel sky, not long wet, not long dry

★

When spiders' webs do fly
The spell will soon be very dry

★

When swallow fly low rain is near

★

A ring round the moon
It will rain very soon

★

Rainbow to windward, foul fall the day,
Rainbow to leeward, damp runs away

★

When the wind veers against the sun
Trust it not, for back 'twill run

For EU product safety concerns, contact us at Calle de José Abascal, 56–1°,
28003 Madrid, Spain or eugpsr@cambridge.org.

www.ingramcontent.com/pod-product-compliance
Ingram Content Group UK Ltd.
Pitfield, Milton Keynes, MK11 3LW, UK
UKHW012327130625
459647UK00009B/118